STAND OUT 3

Evidence-Based Learning for Life, College, and Career

FOURTH EDITION

STACI JOHNSON

ROB JENKINS

NATIONAL GEOGRAPHIC
LEARNING

Australia • Brazil • Canada • Mexico • Singapore • United Kingdom • United States

NATIONAL GEOGRAPHIC LEARNING

National Geographic Learning,
a Cengage Company

Stand Out 3: Evidence-based Learning for Life, College, and Career, Fourth Edition
Staci Johnson, Rob Jenkins

Publisher: Sherrise Roehr

Executive Editor: Sarah Kenney

Senior Development Editor: Margarita Matte

Director of Global Marketing: Ian Martin

Heads of Regional Marketing:

  Charlotte Ellis (Europe, Middle East and Africa

  Justin Kaley (Asia and Greater China)

  Irina Pereyra (Latin America)

  Joy MacFarland (US and Canada)

Senior Content Project Manager: Beth McNally

Content Project Manager: Beth Houston

Media Researcher: Leila Hishmeh

Art Director: Brenda Carmichael

Operations Support: Hayley Chwazik-Gee,
Katie Lee

Manufacturing Planner: Mary Beth Hennebury

Composition: MPS North America LLC

For permission to use material from this text or product,
submit all requests online at **cengage.com/permissions**
Further permissions questions can be emailed to
permissionrequest@cengage.com

Student's Book
ISBN: 978-0-357-96437-8
Student's Book with the Spark platform
ISBN: 978-0-357-96436-1

National Geographic Learning
200 Pier 4 Boulevard
Boston, MA 02210
USA

Locate your local office at **international.cengage.com/region**

Visit National Geographic Learning online at **ELTNGL.com**
Visit our corporate website at **www.cengage.com**

Printed in China
Print Number: 01 Print Year: 2023

Acknowledgments

Mai Ackerman
Ventura College; Los Angeles Mission College, CA

Raul Adalpe
Tarrant County College, Paradise, TX

Mariam Aintablian
Los Angeles Valley College, Valley Glen, CA

Steven Amos
Norfolk Public Schools/Adult Education Services, VA

Ana Arieli
College of Southern Nevada, Las Vegas, NV

Rachel Baiyor
Literacy Outreach, Glenwood Springs, CO

Gregory Baranoff
Santa Barbara City College, Santa Barbara, CA

Valerie Bare
Chesterfield County Public Schools, VA

Dyani Bartlett
Edmonds College, Lynnwood, WA

Karin Bates
Immigrant and Refugee Center of Northern Colorado, CO

Robin Bitters
*Adult Learning Program, Jamaica Plain Community
Center, Putney, VT*

Emily Bryson
*ELT Specialist, Author, Teacher, Teacher Trainer, Graphic
Facilitator, ESOL Lecturer*

Janelle Cardenas
Tarrant County College, TX

Joyce Clement
Chesterfield County Public Schools, VA

Juan Corona
Antelope Valley Adult School, Palmdale, CA

Vasilika Culaku
Goodwill, King County, Seattle, WA

Melinda Dart
Chesterfield County Public Schools, VA

Lourdes Davenport
Tarrant County College, TX

Geisa Dennis
Orange County Public Schools, Orlando, FL

Katie Donoviel
English Skills Learning Center, UT

Reyye Esat Yalcin
Bilingual Education Institute, Houston, TX

Aimee Finley
Dallas College, Dallas, TX

Eleanor Forfang-Brockman
Tarrant County College, Fort Worth, TX

Martha Fredendall
Literacy Outreach, Glenwood Springs, CO

Maria Gutierrez
Miami Sunset Adult Education Center, Miami, FL

Anne Henderson
Goodwill, King County, Seattle, WA

Tracey Higgins
Edmonds College, Lynnwood, WA

Daniel Hopkins
Tarrant County College, TX

Fayne Johnson
*Atlantic Technical College, Arthur Ashe Jr. Campus,
Fort Lauderdale, FL*

Angela Kosmas
City Colleges of Chicago, Chicago, IL

John Kruse
University of Maryland, Arnold, MD

Neskys Liriano
New York Mets, Port Saint Lucie, FL

Maria Manikoth
Snohomish County Goodwill Job Training and Education Center, Everett, WA

Sean McCroskey
Goodwill, King County, Seattle, WA

Yvonne McMahon
Houston Community College, Houston, TX

Xavier Munoz
Literacy Council of Northern Virginia, Falls Church, VA

Sarah Moussavi
Chaffey College, Rancho Cucamonga, CA
Luba Nesterova
Bilingual Education Institute, Houston, TX

Melody Nguyen
Tarrant County College, Arlington, TX

Joseph Ntumba
Goodwill, King County, Seattle, WA

Sachiko Oates
Santa Barbara City College, Santa Barbara, CA

Liane Okamitsu
McKinley Community School for Adults, Honolulu, HI

Dana Orozco
Sweetwater Union High School District, Chula Vista, CA

Betty Osako
McKinley School For Adults, HI

Dr. Sergei Paromchik
Adult Education Hillsborough County Public Schools, Miami, FL

Ileana Perez
Robert Morgan Tech. College, Miami, FL

Carina Raetz
Academy School District 20, Colorado Springs, CO

Tom Randolph
Notre Dame Education Center, Lawrence, MA

Jody Roy
Notre Dame Education Center, Lawrence, MA

Andrew Sansone
Families for Literacy, Saint Peter's University, Jersey City, NJ

Lea Schultz
Lompoc Adult School and Career Center, Lompoc, CA

Jenny Siegfried
Waubonsee Community College, Aurora, IL

Daina Smudrins
Shoreline Community College, Shoreline, WA

Stephanie Sommers
Minneapolis Adult Education, Robbinsdale, MN

Bonnie Taylor
Genesis Center, RI

Yinebeb T. Tessema
Goodwill, King County, Seattle, WA

Dr. Jacqueline Torres
South Dade Senior High, Homestead, FL

Cristina Urena
Atlantic Technical College, Coconut Creek, FL

Marcos Valle
Edmonds College, Lynnwood, WA

Ricardo Vieira Stanton
Bilingual Education Institute, Houston, TX

Lauren Wilson
Shoreline Community College, Shoreline, WA

Pamela Wilson
Palm Beach County Adult and Community Education, FL

ROB JENKINS

STACI JOHNSON

We believe that there's nothing more incredible than the exchange of teaching and learning that goes on in an ESL classroom. And seeing the expression on a student's face when the light goes on reminds us that there's nothing more rewarding than helping a student succeed.

Throughout our careers, we have watched as students rise to challenges and succeed where they were not sure success was possible. Seeing their confidence grow and skills develop brings great joy to both of us and it motivates us to find better ways to reach and support them. We are humbled to think that our contributions to the field over the last 20 years have made a small difference in both students' and teachers' lives. We hope our refinements in ongoing editions will further support their growth and success.

At its core, **Stand Out** has always prioritized robust, relevant content that will deliver student gains in the classroom; while that core mission has not changed, how the program achieves it has certainly evolved in response to changing educational landscape. The basic principles that have made **Stand Out** successful have not changed. Students are challenged to collaborate and think critically through a well-organized series of scaffolded activities that lead to student application in each lesson. The popular first-of-their-kind lesson plans are still prominent. Features such as project-based learning, video, online workbooks, multilevel worksheets, and classroom presentation tools continue to support the core series. New to the fourth edition is explicit workplace exploration. A lesson in each unit has been added to explore different fields and careers, potential salaries, skills, and characteristics which workers might have to excel in potential jobs. Also new to the fourth edition, students will be introduced to *Life Online* in tips, activities, and video throughout the series. In addition, **Stand Out** will now be available in different digital formats compatible with different devices. Finally, **Stand Out** introduces a literacy level that will give access through a unique systematic approach to students who struggle to participate. We believe that with these innovations and features the fourth edition will bring success to every student.

STAND OUT MISSION STATEMENT

Our goal is to inspire students through challenging opportunities to be successful in their language learning experience, so they develop confidence and become independent lifelong learners preparing them for work, school, and life.

Scope and Sequence

UNIT	LESSON 1	LESSON 2	LESSON 3
PRE-UNIT **Getting to Know You** *Page 2*	**Goal:** Introduce yourself and greet others **Grammar:** Present tense; Contractions	**Goal:** Write about yourself **Grammar:** Simple past **Review:** Present continuous **Academic:** Write a paragraph **Life Online:** Paragraph formatting; Tips for online classes	**Goal:** Identify goals **Academic:** Compare and contrast; Set goals **Writing:** Description of goals
1 **Balancing Your Life** *Page 12*	**Goal:** Analyze and create schedules **Grammar:** Adverbs of frequency **Pronunciation:** Stress **Life Online:** Calendar apps **Academic:** Create a schedule	**Goal:** Identify goals and obstacles, and suggest solutions **Grammar:** Future time clauses with *when* **Writing:** Listing goals **Academic:** Active reading; Focused listening	**Goal:** Write about a personal goal **Writing:** Write a paragraph
2 **Consumer Smarts** *Page 38*	**Goal:** Identify places to purchase goods and services **Grammar:** *get* + past participle (causative)	**Goal:** Interpret advertisements **Life Online:** Online purchases	**Goal:** Compare products **Academic:** Compare and contrast **Grammar:** Comparatives; Superlatives

Goal: Analyze study habits **Academic:** Active reading; Inference	**Goal:** Manage time **Academic:** Interpret a pie chart; Focused listening **Academic:** Complete an outline; Focused listening	**Workforce Goal:** Learn about character traits important for work **Academic:** Read an infographic **Workforce:** Understand career clusters **Civics:** Acquiring and evaluating information **Academic:** Skim	**Goal:** Make a schedule **Soft Skill:** Collaboration: Sharing ideas	*A Dreamer* **Academic:** Read for specific information
Goal: Identify and compare purchasing methods **Life Online:** Online payments **Grammar:** Modals: *have to* and *must*	**Goal:** Make a smart purchase **Academic:** Create a sequence **Writing:** Sequencing transition words	**Workforce Goal:** Learn about sales and marketing careers **Academic:** Interpret a pie chart	**Goal:** Two advertisements and a purchase plan **Soft Skill:** Presentation: Plan your presentation	*Rising to the Challenge* **Academic:** Read for understanding

Scope and Sequence

UNIT	LESSON 1	LESSON 2	LESSON 3
3 **Housing** *Page 64*	**Goal:** Interpret classified ads **Grammar:** Comparatives and superlatives using nouns **Academic:** Scan for details	**Goal:** Make decisions **Grammar:** Review: *Yes / No* questions and answers with *do* **Pronunciation:** *Yes / No* Questions	**Goal:** Arrange and cancel utilities **Life Online:** Paperless bills **Grammar:** Review information questions
4 **Our Community** *Page 90*	**Goal:** Ask for information **Grammar:** Information questions **Life Online:** Research information **Pronunciation:** Information Questions	**Goal:** Interpret charts and compare information **Life Online:** Useful banking tips **Academic:** Interpret online information	**Goal:** Use map apps **Academic:** Read a map; Understand systems **Civics:** Public services

Life Online Video *Page 116*

UNIT	LESSON 1	LESSON 2	LESSON 3
5 **Health** *Page 118*	**Goal:** Identify parts of the body **Academic:** Make recommendations **Grammar:** Modal *should*	**Goal:** Communicate symptoms **Grammar:** Present perfect; *For* and *since*	**Goal:** Identify and analyze health habits **Grammar:** Future conditional **Academic:** Reflect on habits

LESSON 4	LESSON 5	LESSON 6	TEAM PROJECT	READING CHALLENGE
Goal: Create a budget **Academic:** Budget arithmetic; Read a bar graph **Life Online:** Getting the best deal	**Goal:** Write a formal letter **Grammar:** Past continuous + *while* **Writing:** A formal email	**Workforce Goal:** Compare property management careers **Academic:** Evaluate a bar graph	**Goal:** Create a housing plan **Soft Skill:** Active Listening: Listen attentively	*Tiny House Living* **Academic:** Active reading; Make inferences
Goal: Identify daily activities **Academic:** Focused listening **Grammar:** Adverbial clauses with *before*, *after*, and *when* **Pronunciation:** Pausing	**Goal:** Describe a place **Academic:** Write a paragraph **Writing:** Transitions	**Workforce Goal:** Compare careers in banking **Academic:** Interpret data	**Goal:** Create a community brochure **Soft Skill:** Active listening: Listen carefully	*Giving Back* **Academic:** Identify synonyms
Goal: Analyze nutrition information **Review:** Imperatives **Academic:** Active listening	**Goal:** Interpret fitness information **Life Online:** Step counter apps	**Workforce Goal:** Compare health-related careers **Academic:** Understand charts **Writing:** Write about career preference	**Goal:** Create a healthy-living plan **Soft Skill:** Collaboration: Express disagreements politely	*Blue Zones* **Academic:** Active reading, Word connotations

Scope and Sequence

UNIT	LESSON 1	LESSON 2	LESSON 3
6 **Getting Hired** *Page 144*	**Goal:** Identify job titles and skills **Life Online:** Research using key words **Grammar:** Review simple present **Writing:** Job skills	**Goal:** Identify job skills and personality traits **Grammar:** Infinitives and Gerunds; Gerunds and nouns after prepositions	**Goal:** Interpret job advertisements **Academic:** Active reading **Writing:** Create an ad
7 **On the Job** *Page 170*	**Goal:** Compare employee behavior and attitudes **Academic:** Focused listening **Grammar:** Possessive adjectives and possessive pronouns	**Goal:** Interpret a pay stub **Academic:** Read for understanding; Make calculations	**Goal:** Analyze benefit information **Academic:** Focused listening **Life Online:** Technology at work
8 **Citizens and Community** *Page 196*	**Goal:** Identify US geographical locations **Civic:** Find information in a map **Academic:** Focused listening	**Goal:** Compare and contrast ideas **Grammar:** Comparing and contrasting ideas	**Goal:** Compare the branches of US government **Civic:** Understand functions of government officials **Writing:** Write about job preferences

Life Online Video *Page 222*

LESSON 4	LESSON 5	LESSON 6	TEAM PROJECT	READING CHALLENGE
Goal: Complete a job application **Life Online:** Professional social media sites **Academic:** Understanding forms	**Goal:** Interview for a job **Grammar:** *Would rather*	**Workforce Goal:** Discover a career in general management **Academic:** Understand statistics	**Goal:** Create a job ad for a job fair **Soft Skill:** Collaboration: Brainstorm ideas **Life Online:** Collaboration tools	*Should You Learn a Trade?* **Civics:** Learn about pay in the trades **Academic:** Scan for details
Goal: Identify safe workplace behavior **Grammar:** *Could* and *might*	**Goal:** Communicate at work **Academic:** Focused listening **Grammar:** Polite requests and responses **Pronunciation:** Rising intonation for polite requests	**Workforce Goal:** Discover human resources jobs **Academic:** Interpret information	**Goal:** Create an employee handbook **Soft Skill:** Collaboration: Polite suggestions	*Know Your Rights* **Academic:** Read for understanding
Goal: Express opinions **Grammar:** Modal *should* **Life Online:** Municipal apps	**Goal:** Write a speech **Grammar:** Conditional statements **Writing:** Expressing opinions	**Workforce Goal:** Learn about careers in local government **Academic:** Read a bar graph; Conduct a poll	**Goal:** Run for mayor **Soft Skill:** Presentation: Public speaking	*Time for a Change* **Academic:** Scan for details

NEW AND UPDATED IN *STAND OUT*, FOURTH EDITION

Now in its fourth edition, *Stand Out* is a seven-level, standards-based adult education program with a track record of real-world results. Close alignment to WIOA objectives and College and Career Readiness Standards provides adult students with language and skills for success in the workplace, college, and everyday life.

New Literacy level

**The Literacy level follows an instructional design that meets the needs of lower-level English learners.

Each unit opens with a dynamic image to introduce the theme and engage learners in meaningful conversations from the start.

New **'Life Online'** sections develop digital literacy skills.

An **updated video program** now features two 'Life Online' videos with related practice that aligns with workforce and digital literacy objectives.

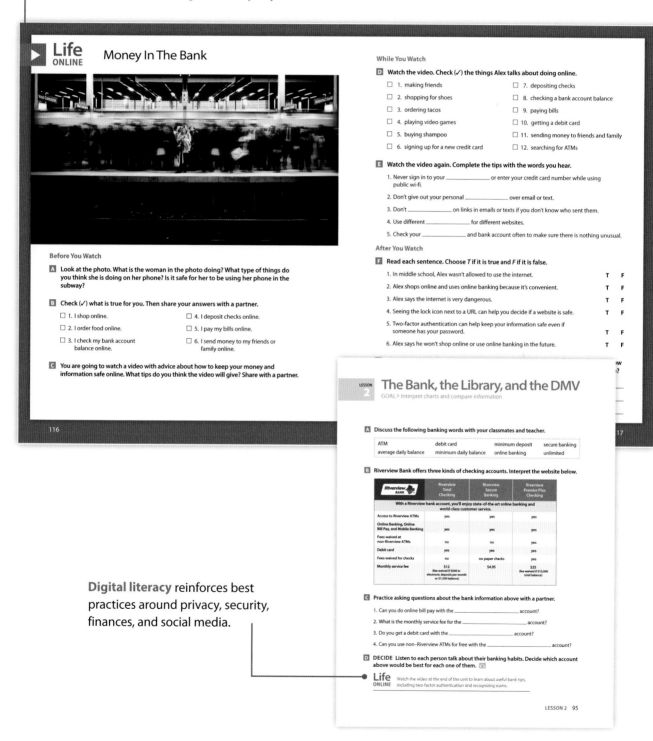

Life ONLINE — Money In The Bank

Before You Watch

A Look at the photo. What is the woman in the photo doing? What type of things do you think she is doing on her phone? Is it safe for her to be using her phone in the subway?

B Check (✓) what is true for you. Then share your answers with a partner.

☐ 1. I shop online.
☐ 2. I order food online.
☐ 3. I check my bank account balance online.
☐ 4. I deposit checks online.
☐ 5. I pay my bills online.
☐ 6. I send money to my friends or family online.

C You are going to watch a video with advice about how to keep your money and information safe online. What tips do you think the video will give? Share with a partner.

116

While You Watch

D Watch the video. Check (✓) the things Alex talks about doing online.

☐ 1. making friends
☐ 2. shopping for shoes
☐ 3. ordering tacos
☐ 4. playing video games
☐ 5. buying shampoo
☐ 6. signing up for a new credit card
☐ 7. depositing checks
☐ 8. checking a bank account balance
☐ 9. paying bills
☐ 10. getting a debit card
☐ 11. sending money to friends and family
☐ 12. searching for ATMs

E Watch the video again. Complete the tips with the words you hear.

1. Never sign in to your _____ or enter your credit card number while using public wi-fi.

2. Don't give out your personal _____ over email or text.

3. Don't _____ on links in emails or texts if you don't know who sent them.

4. Use different _____ for different websites.

5. Check your _____ and bank account often to make sure there is nothing unusual.

After You Watch

F Read each sentence. Choose *T* if it is true and *F* if it is false.

	T	F
1. In middle school, Alex wasn't allowed to use the internet.	T	F
2. Alex shops online and uses online banking because it's convenient.	T	F
3. Alex says the internet is very dangerous.	T	F
4. Seeing the lock icon next to a URL can help you decide if a website is safe.	T	F
5. Two-factor authentication can help keep your information safe even if someone has your password.	T	F
6. Alex says he won't shop online or use online banking in the future.	T	F

17

Digital literacy reinforces best practices around privacy, security, finances, and social media.

LESSON 2 — The Bank, the Library, and the DMV

GOAL ▶ Interpret charts and compare information

A Discuss the following banking words with your classmates and teacher.

ATM	debit card	minimum deposit	secure banking
average daily balance	minimum daily balance	online banking	unlimited

B Riverview Bank offers three kinds of checking accounts. Interpret the website below.

Riverview BANK	Riverview Total Checking	Riverview Secure Banking	Riverview Premier Plus Checking
With a Riverview bank account, you'll enjoy state-of-the-art online banking and world-class customer service.			
Access to Riverview ATMs	yes	yes	yes
Online Banking, Online Bill Pay, and Mobile Banking	yes	yes	yes
Fees waived at non-Riverview ATMs	no	no	yes
Debit card	yes	yes	yes
Fees waived for checks	no	no paper checks	yes
Monthly service fee	$12 (fee waived if $500 in electronic deposits per month or $1,500 balance)	$4.95	$25 (fee waived if $15,000 total balance)

C Practice asking questions about the bank information above with a partner.

1. Can you do online bill pay with the _____ account?
2. What is the monthly service fee for the _____ account?
3. Do you get a debit card with the _____ account?
4. Can you use non–Riverview ATMs for free with the _____ account?

D **DECIDE** Listen to each person talk about their banking habits. Decide which account above would be best for each one of them. 🔊

Life ONLINE — Watch the video at the end of the unit to learn about useful bank tips, including two-factor authentication and recognizing scams.

LESSON 2 95

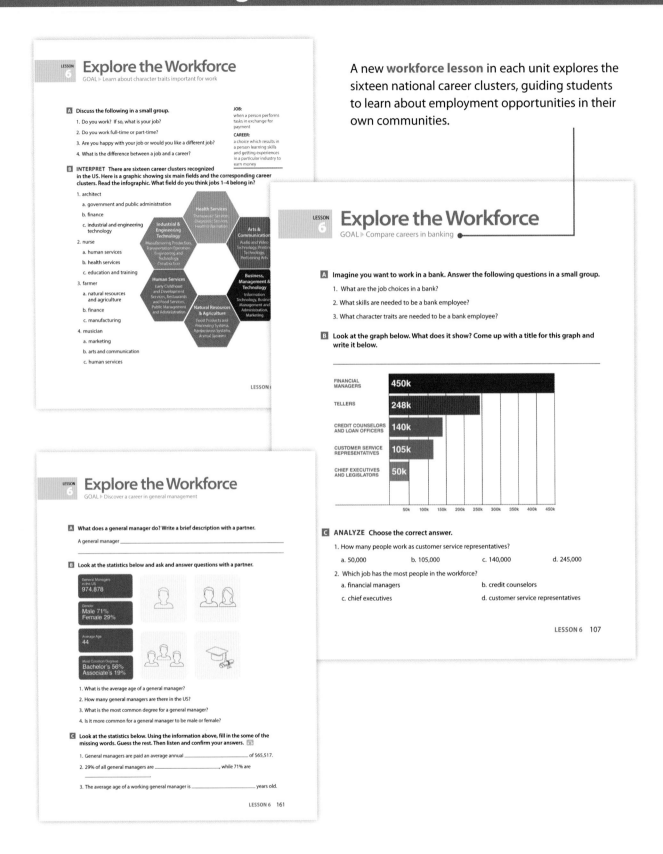

A new **workforce lesson** in each unit explores the sixteen national career clusters, guiding students to learn about employment opportunities in their own communities.

Team Project

Create a Community Brochure

SOFT SKILL ▶ Active listening

Imagine that a new family has moved into your neighborhood and you want to tell them all about your community. With your team, create a brochure about your community.

1. Form a team of four or five students. Choose a position for each member of your team.

Position	Job Description	Student Name(s)
Student 1: Leader	Check that everyone speaks English. Check that everyone participates.	
Student 2: Writer	Write information for brochure with help from the team.	
Student 3: Designer	Design brochure layout and add artwork.	
Students 4/5: City Representatives	Help writer and designer with their work.	

2. Make a list of everything you want to include in your brochure, for example: information about the library, banks, and other local services.

3. Create the text for your community brochure.

4. Create a map of your community. Then create artwork for your community brochure.

5. Present your brochure to the class.

Active Listening
Listen carefully
Listen carefully while each team is presenting. How is their presentation different than yours? How is it the same?

Public sculptures, like The Bean in Chicago, are great places for people to meet in towns and cities.

*Team projects now highlight transferrable **Soft Skills**, such as collaboration, active listening, and presentation skills.*

*The fully updated **Reading Challenge** will expose students to CASAS STEPS test question types.*

Reading Challenge

A PREDICT Look at the company's logo in the photo. What do you think it is a picture of? What types of food and drink do you think they serve at this café?

B Match the vocabulary word to its correct meaning.

_____ 1. brunch   a. money that a person gets if he or she loses his or her job

_____ 2. pandemic   b. evidence that something is true

_____ 3. unemployment   c. a meal that combines breakfast and lunch

_____ 4. proof   d. a disease that happens to people all over the world

C Read the text.

D SEQUENCE Put the events in the correct order.

_____ Carolina collected unemployment.

___1___ Carolina lived in Guatemala City.

_____ Carolina lost her job.

_____ Carolina worked as a housekeeper.

_____ Carolina built her café.

_____ Carolina found a chef and business partner.

_____ Carolina crossed the border with her mother.

_____ Carolina opened Tikal Café.

E On a separate piece of paper, rewrite the sentences in D in the correct order, adding in extra details from the text. Sometimes, change the name Carolina to "she" to avoid too much repetition and add transitions like *such as*, *then*, *next*, etc.

EXAMPLE: Carolina lived in Guatemala City. In 2008, she came to the US with her mother. Then...

F EXPAND Imagine you are planning a visit to Brooklyn for brunch. What would you order?

Rising to the Challenge

Tikal Café is a brunch and coffee shop located in Brooklyn, New York. If you go to its website, you will see delicious menu items such as Avocado Toast, Winter Porridge, a Walnut Pesto Quesadilla and Coconut Yogurt. You can drink Matcha, Iced Lavender Lattes, or Cold Brew Coffee. But what you won't see on the website is that the café is owned by an immigrant,
5   Carolina Hernandez from Guatemala.

Carolina is from Guatemala City, Guatemala, and came to the US with her mother in 2008. For over 10 years, she worked two to three jobs so she could save up enough money to open her own business. Sometimes, she worked 18-hour days. She used the money from her housekeeping job to survive and pay her bills. And she used the money from her food serving
10   job to save for her dream.

Unfortunately, when the pandemic hit in 2020, she lost all of her jobs. She was able to collect unemployment, but she wasn't happy. Carolina was a hard worker and wanted to work to earn her money, not sit on the couch and watch Netflix. So, she found a business partner, who is now the chef at the café, and picked out a location close to her home. She started with
15   an empty space and eventually built Tikal Café, a neighborhood spot where locals can come to enjoy a cup of coffee and a delicious meal. From housekeeper to restaurant owner—Carolina is living proof of the American Dream.

Carolina Hernandez's hard work made her dream come true.

spark

Bring *Stand Out* to life with the Spark platform — where you can prepare, teach and assess your classes all in one place!

Manage your course and teach great classes with integrated digital teaching and learning tools. Spark brings together everything you need on an all-in-one platform with a single log-in.

Track student and class performance on independent online practice and assessment, including CASAS practice. The Course Gradebook helps you turn information into insights to make the most of valuable classroom time.

Set up classes and roster students quickly and easily on Spark. Seamless integration options and point-of-use support helps you focus on what matters most: student success.

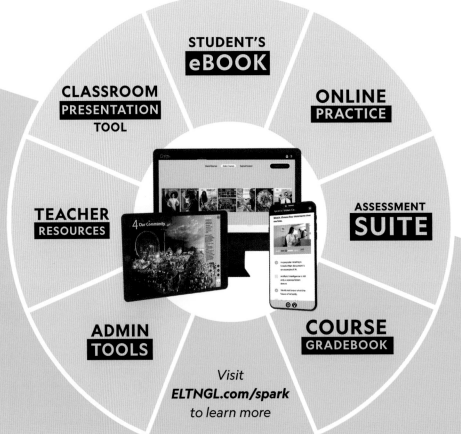

STUDENT'S
eBOOK

CLASSROOM
PRESENTATION
TOOL

ONLINE
PRACTICE

TEACHER
RESOURCES

ASSESSMENT
SUITE

ADMIN
TOOLS

COURSE
GRADEBOOK

Visit
ELTNGL.com/spark
to learn more

CASAS Correlation Chart

PRE-UNIT Getting to Know You	
Lesson 1: Introduce yourself and greet others	0.1.2, 0.1.5, 0.2.1, 0.2.2
Lesson 2: Write about yourself	0.1.2, 0.1.5, 0.2.1
Lesson 3: Identify goals	0.1.6, 0.2.1, 7.1.1, 7.4.4, 7.4.8, 7.7.3

Unit 1 Balancing Your Life	
Lesson 1: Analyze and create schedules	0.1.2, 0.1.5, 0.2.4
Lesson 2: Identify goals and obstacles and suggest solutions	0.1.2, 0.1.5, 7.1.1, 7.1.2, 7.1.3, 7.2.5, 7.2.6, 7.2.7
Lesson 3: Write about a personal goal	0.1.2, 0.1.5, 7.1.1, 7.1.2, 7.1.3, 7.2.5, 7.2.6, 7.2.7, 7.3.4
Lesson 4: Analyze study habits	0.1.2, 0.1.5, 7.4.1, 7.4.3
Lesson 5: Manage time	0.1.2, 0.1.5, 6.7.4, 7.4.1, 7.5.5
Lesson 6: Learn about character traits important for work	0.1.2, 0.1.5, 4.1.3, 4.1.6, 7.4.4, 7.4.8, 7.7.3
Review	0.1.2, 0.1.5, 7.1.1, 7.2.7, 7.4.1, 7.4.3
Team Project	0.1.2, 0.1.5, 4.8.1, 4.8.5, 7.1.1, 7.1.2, 7.2.6, 7.2.7, 7.4.1, 7.5.5
Reading Challenge	0.2.3

Unit 2 Consumer Smarts	
Lesson 1: Identifying places to purchase goods and services	0.1.2, 0.1.5, 1.2.6, 7.4.4, 7.7.3
Lesson 2: Interpret advertisements	0.1.2, 0.1.5, 1.2.1, 1.2.3, 1.2.5, 7.4.4, 7.7.3
Lesson 3: Compare products	0.1.2, 0.1.5, 1.2.2
Lesson 4: Identify and compare purchasing methods	0.1.2, 0.1.5, 1.2.1, 1.2.2, 1.3.1
Lesson 5: Make a smart purchase	1.2.2. 1.3.1
Lesson 6: Explore sales and marketing careers	0.1.2, 0.1.5, 4.1.3, 4.1.6, 6.7.4, 7.4.4, 7.4.8, 7.7.3
Review	1.2.1, 1.2.2, 1.3.1
Team Project	0.1.2, 0.1.5, 1.2.2, 1,3.1, 4.8.1, 4.8.5
Reading Challenge	7.4.4, 7.7.3

Unit 3 Housing	
Lesson 1: Interpret classified ads	0.1.2, 0.1.5, 1.4.1, 1.4.2, 7.4.4, 7.7.3
Lesson 2: Make decisions	0.1.2, 0.1.5, 1.4.1, 7.2.7
Lesson 3: Arrange and cancel utilities	0.1.2, 0.1.5, 1.4.4, 1.5.3
Lesson 4: Create a budget	0.1.2, 0.1.5, 1.1.6, 1.5.1, 6.0.3, 6.1.1, 6.1.2, 6.7.2
Lesson 5: Write a formal letter	0.1.2, 0.1.5, 0.2.3, 1.4.7, 7.2.7
Lesson 6: Compare Property Management Careers	0.1.2, 0.1.5, 4.1.3, 4.1.6, 4.8.1, 6.7.3
Review	0.1.2, 0.1.5, 0.2.3, 1.4.2, 1.4.4, 1.4.7, 1.5.1, 6.0.3, 6.1.1
Team Project	0.1.2, 0.1.5, 1.4.2, 1.5.1, 4.8.1, 4.8.5
Reading Challenge	1.4.1, 1.4.2, 7.4.4, 7.7.3

Unit 4 Our Community	
Lesson 1: Ask for information	0.1.2, 0.1.5
Lesson 2: Interpret charts and compare information	0.1.2, 0.1.5, 1.8.3, 2.5.6, 7.4.8
Lesson 3: Interpret a road map	0.1.2, 0.1.5, 2.2.1, 2.2.5
Lesson 4: Identify daily activities	0.1.2, 0.1.5, 0.2.4, 7.2.6
Lesson 5: Describe a place	7.2.6
Lesson 6: Compare careers in banking	0.1.2, 0.1.5, 4.1.3, 4.1.6, 4.8.1, 6.7.2
Review	0.1.2, 0.1.5, 1.8.3, 2.2.1, 2.2.5
Team Project	0.1.2, 0.1.5, 2.2.5, 4.8.1, 4.8.5
Reading Challenge	0.1.2, 0.1.5

Unit 5 Health	
Lesson 1: Identify parts of the human body	0.1.2, 0.1.5, 3.6.1
Lesson 2: Communicate symptoms	0.1.2, 0.1.5, 3.6.3
Lesson 3: Identify and analyze health habits	0.1.2, 0.1.5, 3.4.2, 3.5.9
Lesson 4: Analyze nutrition information	0.1.2, 0.1.5, 3.5.1, 3.5.3, 3.5.5, 3.5.9, 6.7.3
Lesson 5: Interpret fitness information	0.1.2, 0.1.5, 3.5.9
Lesson 6: Compare health-related careers	0.1.2, 0.1.5, 4.1.3, 4.1.6, 4.8.1, 6.7.2
Review	3.5.9, 3.6.3
Team Project	0.1.2, 0.1.5, 3.6.3, 4.8.1, 4.8.5
Reading Challenge	0.1.2, 0.1.5, 3.5.2, 3.5.9

Unit 6 Getting Hired	
Lesson 1: Identify job titles and skills	0.1.2, 0.1.5, 4.1.8
Lesson 2: Identify job skills and personality traits	0.1.2, 0.1.5, 4.1.8, 4.1.9
Lesson 3: Interpret job advertisements	4.1.3, 4.1.8, 4.1.9
Lesson 4: Complete a job application	0.1.2, 0.1.5, 4.1.2
Lesson 5: Interview for a job	0.1.2, 0.1.5, 4.1.5, 4.1.7
Lesson 6: Discover a career in general management	0.1.2, 0.1.5, 4.1.3, 4.1.6, 4.8.1, 6.7.2, 6.7.3
Review	4.1.2, 4.1.3, 4.1.8, 4.1.9, 7.4.5
Team Project	0.1.2, 0.1.5, 4.1.3, 4.8.1, 4.8.5, 7.2.6
Reading Challenge	4.1.8

Unit 7 On the Job	
Lesson 1: Compare employee behavior and attitude	0.1.2, 0.1.5, 4.1.9, 4.4.1
Lesson 2: Interpret a pay stub	0.1.2, 0.1.5, 4.2.1
Lesson 3: Analyze benefit information	0.1.2, 0.1.5, 4.2.1
Lesson 4: Identify safe workplace behavior	0.1.2, 0.1.5, 4.2.5
Lesson 5: Communicate at work	0.1.2, 0.1.5, 4.4.1, 4.6.1, 4.7.3
Lesson 6: Discover Human Resources Jobs	0.1.2, 0.1.5, 4.1.3, 4.1.6, 4.1.8, 4.1.9, 4.8.1, 6.7.3, 6.7.4
Review	0.1.2, 0.1.5, 4.2.1, 4.2.5, 4.6.1, 7.4.5
Team Project	0.1.2, 0.1.5, 4.2.4, 4.2.5, 4.8.1, 4.8.5
Reading Challenge	4.2.6

Unit 8 Citizens and Community	
Lesson 1: Identify U.S. geographical locations	0.1.2, 0.1.5, 5.2.4, 5.2.6
Lesson 2: Compare and contrast ideas	0.1.2, 0.1.5, 5.1.4, 5.1.6, 5.5.8
Lesson 3: Interpret the branches of the U.S. government	0.1.2, 0.1.5, 5.5.2, 5.5.3, 5.5.4, 5.5.8, 5.5.9
Lesson 4: Express opinions	0.1.2, 0.1.5, 7.3.1, 7.3.2, 7.3.4
Lesson 5: Write a speech	0.1.2, 0.1.5, 5.1.6, 5.5.8, 5.5.9
Lesson 6: Learn about careers in local government	0.1.2, 0.1.5, 4.1.3, 4.1.6, 4.1.8, 4.1.9, 4.8.1, 6.7.2
Review	5.2.4, 5.5.2, 5.5.3, 5.5.4 , 7.3.1, 7.3.2, 7.3.4
Team Project	0.1.2, 0.1.5, 5.1.4, 7.3.1, 7.3.2, 73.4, 4.8.1, 4.8.5
Reading Challenge	5.2.4, 5.5.8

For more correlations, including ELPS, CCRS, and ELCivics, visit the Spark Platform.

PRE-UNIT

Getting to Know You

UNIT OUTCOMES

▶ Introduce yourself and greet others

▶ Write about yourself

▶ Identify goals

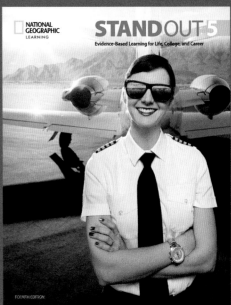

Nice to Meet You!

GOAL ▶ Introduce yourself and greet others

A Complete the school registration form.

SANTA ANA ADULT SCHOOL

REGISTRATION FORM

First Name   Middle Initial   Last Name

Address:

Number and Street

City   State   Zip

Phone: Home ☐   Cell ☐

Email Address   Date of Birth (mm/dd/yyyy)

Languages Spoken

Occupation

B Write three questions to ask your classmates about the information on their registration forms.

EXAMPLE: What is your first name?

1. _____

2. _____

3. _____

C SURVEY Write your questions from **B** in the table and interview two classmates. Use the conversations below as models.

You:	What is your <u>first name</u>?
Student A:	My first name is Michel.
You:	Where are you from?
Student A:	I'm from Haiti.
You:	What's your <u>first name</u>?
Student B:	My first name is Selma.
You:	Where are you from?
Student B:	I'm from Brazil.

Contractions 🎧

What is = *What's*
What's your name?

Question	Student A	Student B

D Introduce the two classmates you interviewed to the rest of the class.

EXAMPLE: This is Michel. His last name is Caron. He is from Haiti.
This is Selma. Her last name is Bezerra. She's from Brazil.

E Juan and Michel take English class together. Read and practice their conversation.

Juan: Good morning.

Michel: Morning!

Juan: How are you today?

Michel: Great! How about you?

Juan: Fine, thanks.

F Listen to the greetings and possible responses. 🎧

Greetings	Possible Responses
Hi!	Hello!
Good morning!	Morning!
How are you today?	Fine. / Great!
How's it going?	Pretty good.
How are you doing?	OK. / Not bad.
What's up?	Nothing.
What's new?	Not much.

Online Greeting Situations	Possible Responses
mouth moves, no sound	You're muted!
Type 'hi' in the chat box	Type 'hi' back in the chat box

G Listen to the greetings and respond after each one. 🎧

H **APPLY** Greet three different classmates. Ask them a few personal information questions like the ones you wrote in **B**.

There are many different ways to accompany a greeting. In the United States, the most common is a handshake.

Tell Your Story

GOAL ▶ Write about yourself

A **Read about Akiko.** 🎧

Santa Ana is the second largest city in Orange County, California.

My name is Akiko Sugiyama. We live in Santa Ana, California. I'm a student at Santa Ana Adult School. I came to the United States five years ago from Japan with my husband and three children. My husband works in a computer assembly factory. I go to school and take care of our children. We are both studying English because we want to be successful in this country. Someday we hope to buy a house and send our children to college.

B **Answer the questions about Akiko.**

1. When did Akiko come to the United States? _____

2. Where is she from? _____

3. Who did she come to the United States with? _____

4. Where does she live? _____

5. What does her husband do? _____

6. What does she do? _____

7. Why is she studying English? _____

8. What are her future goals? _____

C **Answer the questions about yourself.**

1. When did you come to this country? _____

2. Where are you from? _____

3. Who did you come to this country with? _____

4. Where do you live? _____

5. What do you do? _____

6. Why are you studying English? _____

7. What are your future goals? _____

D **ANALYZE** **Study the layout of the paragraph.**

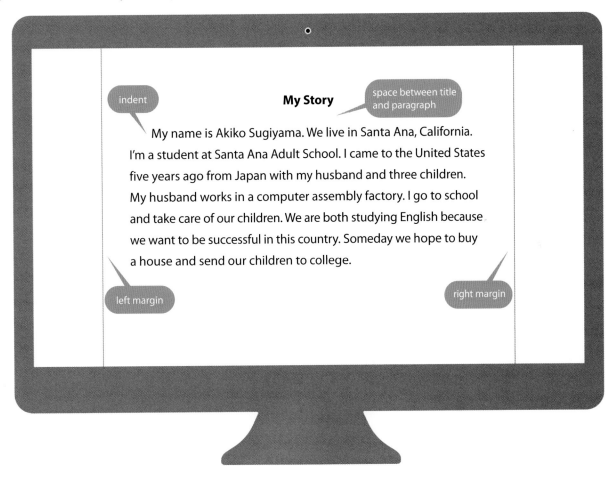

 When you use a computer or tablet to type your paper, there are automatically margins for your writing. But you still have to indent (TAB) your paragraphs and put a blank / empty line (press *Enter*) between your title and the beginning of your paragraph.

E Look at the paragraph below. What is wrong with the formatting? Discuss with a partner.

> **All About Me**
>
> My name is Basel. I'm a new student at Big Pine Adult School. We moved to the United States last year from Afghanistan. I didn't finish high school in my country, so I'm here at the adult school to get my GED. I want to go to a college for computer programming. Someday I would like to make video games.

_____

_____

_____

F COMPOSE Write a paragraph about yourself with the answers you wrote in **C**. Use correct paragraph formatting like in Akiko's paragraph in **D**.

_____

_____

_____

_____

_____

_____

G COMPARE Share your paragraph with a partner. Did your partner use correct paragraph formatting?

TIPS FOR ONLINE CLASSES

1. A breakout room is a place where you can work with a partner online. It's important to understand the assignment before you go into your breakout room, so make sure you ask your teacher questions first.

2. If you are doing this online, make sure to raise your hand online so your teacher can call on you when you're ready to introduce your classmates.

Life
ONLINE

3. Share your work with your class by sharing your screen or holding your book up to the camera for your classmates to see.

Are You College Bound?

GOAL ▶ Identify goals

A This flowchart represents the educational system in the United States. Read the flowchart with your teacher.

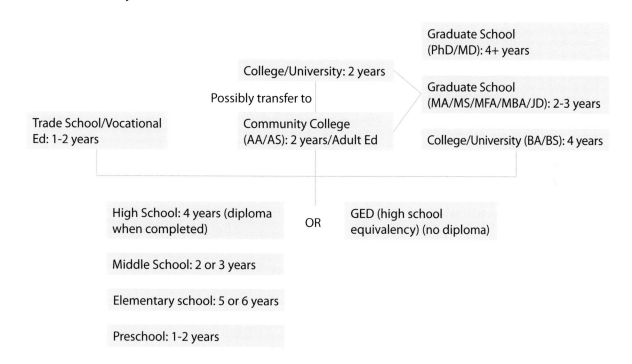

Graduate School
(PhD/MD): 4+ years

College/University: 2 years

Possibly transfer to

Graduate School
(MA/MS/MFA/MBA/JD): 2-3 years

Trade School/Vocational
Ed: 1-2 years

Community College
(AA/AS): 2 years/Adult Ed

College/University (BA/BS): 4 years

High School: 4 years (diploma when completed)

OR

GED (high school equivalency) (no diploma)

Middle School: 2 or 3 years

Elementary school: 5 or 6 years

Preschool: 1-2 years

B **PREDICT** What do the abbreviations in the table stand for and mean? Ask your teacher for help.

Abbreviation	Stands for . . .	Meaning
AA	Associate of Arts	two-year degree from a community college with an art-related major
BA		
BS		
MA		
MS		
PhD		
EdD		

C Go online. What are some other abbreviations for degrees?

D Choose the best answer. Look back at the flowchart if you need help.

1. What is the lowest level of education in the United States?

   a. kindergarten   b. preschool   c. graduate school

2. How many years do students go to high school?

   a. three years   b. two years   c. four years

3. What is the highest degree you can get?

   a. MA   b. MS   c. PhD

4. Where can you get a BA or BS degree?

   a. college   b. graduate school   c. technical college

E **COMPARE** Draw a flowchart to show your country's educational system. Compare your flowchart with a classmate's.

F Check (✓) the educational levels you have completed. Circle the educational level you would like to achieve.

Graduate School (PhD/MD): 4+ years

College/University 1-2 years

Possibly transfer to

Graduate School (MA/MS/MFA/MBA/JD): 3 years

Trade School/Vocational Ed: 1-2 years

Community College (AA/AS): 2 years/Adult Ed

College/University (BA/BS): 4 years

High School: 4 years (diploma when completed)   OR   GED (high school equivalency) (no diploma)

Middle School: 2 or 3 years

Elementary school: 5 or 6 years

Preschool: 1-2 years

G **COMPOSE** How do you plan to achieve your educational goals? Write a paragraph. Write a title for your paragraph.

_____

_____

_____

_____

_____

_____

_____

_____

_____

_____

_____

1 Balancing Your Life

UNIT OUTCOMES

▶ Analyze and create schedules

▶ Identify goals and obstacles, and suggest solutions

▶ Write about a personal goal

▶ Analyze study habits

▶ Manage time

▶ Learn about character traits important for work

Answer the questions.

A young woman practiced yoga at home because yoga centers where closed during the COVID outbreak.

1. What do you do in your free time?

2. What activities do you do every day?

3. How do you balance your free time and activities you do every day?

4. Describe what you see in this photo.

5. Do you think the yoga pose this young woman is doing is difficult? Why?

6. How is this woman balancing her life?

Everyday Life

GOAL ▶ Analyze and create schedules

A *routine* is something you regularly do. For example: Luisa runs four mornings a week. Luisa watches a movie every Saturday at 7 p.m.

A ANALYZE Look at Luisa's schedule. What are her routines?

	Monday	Tuesday	Wednesday	Thursday	Friday	Saturday	Sunday
5 a.m. – 7 a.m.	5:45 Run		5:45 Run		5:45 Run	6:00 Yoga	5:45 Run
7 a.m. – 9 a.m.	7:00 Walk the dog	7:00 Walk the dog	7:00 Walk the dog 8:00 Breakfast with co-workers	7:00 Walk the dog	7:00 Walk the dog	7:00 Walk the dog 8:00 Work	7:00 Walk the dog
9 a.m. – 11 a.m.	9:00 Work	9:00 Grocery shopping	9:00 Work	9:00 Run errands	9:00 Work	10:00 Shopping	
11 a.m. – 1 p.m.							
1 p.m. – 3 p.m.		1:00 Work		1:00 Work		2:00 Meet friends	1:00 Meet friends
3 p.m. – 5 p.m.							
5 p.m. – 7 p.m.							5:00 Family dinner
7 p.m. – 9 p.m.	7:00 ESL class	8:00 Computer class	7:00 ESL class	8:00 Computer class		7:00 Watch a movie	

B Ask questions about Luisa's schedule. Use the conversation below as a model.

Student A: What time does Luisa start work?

Student B: She starts work at 9:00 a.m. on Mondays, Wednesdays, and Fridays.

Student A: When does she have ESL class?

Student B: She has ESL class on Mondays and Wednesdays at 7:00 p.m.

Life ONLINE

There are apps that people use to keep track of their schedule. Do you use a calendar app? What do you use it for? Share.

C **INTERPRET** Ask questions about Luisa's schedule again. This time, use *How often . . . ?* Answer the questions using the frequency expressions from the box.

every morning	every weekday	every Sunday	three times a week
every other day	every Saturday	once a week	twice a week

EXAMPLE: **Student A:**   How often does Luisa have dinner with her family?
                    Student B: Luisa has dinner with her family <u>every Sunday</u>.
                                       Or Luisa has dinner with her family <u>once a week</u>.

D Where do frequency adverbs go in a sentence? Study the charts below.

0%   50%   100%

never   rarely   sometimes   usually   always

Placement Rules for Frequency Adverbs	Examples
Before the main verb	Luisa *always / usually / often* **goes** running. She *sometimes / rarely / never* <u>does</u> yoga.
After the main verb *be*	She <u>is</u> *usually* busy on the weekends.
Sometimes / usually / often can come at the beginning or at the end of a sentence	*Usually / Sometimes,* Luisa starts work in the morning. Luisa starts work in the morning *sometimes / often.*
Between the subject and the verb in short answers	Yes, <u>she</u> *always* <u>does</u>. / No, <u>she</u> *usually* <u>isn't</u>.
Rarely and *never* are negative words. Do not use them with *not.*	Correct: She *never* plays tennis. Incorrect: She ~~doesn't~~ *never* plays tennis.

E Write the frequency adverb in parentheses in the correct place. Remember, sometimes the adverb can go in more than one place.

    rarely
1. Roberto ^finishes his homework before class. (rarely)

2. Jerry comes to class on time. (always)

3. Sue eats lunch with her husband. (sometimes)

4. Our teacher sits at her desk while she is teaching. (never)

5. Elia goes running in the morning before school. (often)

6. Hugo works at night. (usually)

Stress 🎧

In a phrase or sentence, certain words get the most stress.

Luisa OFTEN goes RUNNING.

She is NEVER HOME on the weekends.

SOMETIMES, I go to the MOVIES.

He RARELY studies in the MORNING.

F Use frequency adverbs to write sentences about Luisa. Look back at her schedule in **A**.

1. _Luisa usually starts work in the morning._ _____

2. _____

3. _____

4. _____

G Practice reading the sentences you wrote in **F**. Which words are the most important in each sentence?

H **CREATE** Make a schedule of everything you do in one week. Tell a partner about your schedule.

EXAMPLE: I NEVER cook on my day off because I'm a cook in a restaurant!

	Monday	Tuesday	Wednesday	Thursday	Friday	Saturday	Sunday
5 a.m. – 7 a.m.							
7 a.m. – 9 a.m.							
9 a.m. – 11 a.m.							
11 a.m. – 1 p.m.							
1 p.m. – 3 p.m.							
3 p.m. – 5 p.m.							
5 p.m. – 7 p.m.							
7 p.m. – 9 p.m.							

Goals, Obstacles, and Solutions

GOAL ▶ Identify goals and obstacles, and suggest solutions

A Look at the picture. Bolin is worried about the future. What is he thinking about?

B Read about Bolin. 🎧

    Bolin's life is going to change very soon. His wife, Daiyu, is going to have twins in July. His parents are going to come from China to live in the United States. He's happy, but his apartment will to be too small for everyone. He needs a better job, but his boss *won't* promote him because he doesn't have a college degree.

    Bolin has three goals. When his parents come to the United States, he will buy a house large enough for two families. His father will work and help pay for the house. His mother will help take care of the children. Then Bolin plans to go to night school and get his bachelor's degree. When he graduates, he will apply for a new position at work. He will work hard to achieve his goals.

*won't = will not

C A *goal* is something you would like to achieve in the future. What are Bolin's three goals?

1. _____

2. _____

3. _____

D An *obstacle* is a problem; something that gets in the way of your goal. Bolin has two obstacles. What are they?

1. _____

2. _____

E Review vocabulary and write about Bolin's solutions.

1. What is a goal? _____

2. What is an obstacle? _____

3. What is a solution? *A solution is a way to solve a problem.* _____

4. Bolin's apartment is too small. What is his solution?

_____

5. Bolin needs a better job. What is his solution? _____

_____

F **IDENTIFY** Listen to Tuba and Lam. Identify their goals, obstacles, and solutions and write them in the spaces.

1. **Goal:** Tuba wants to *get a job to help her husband* _____.

Obstacle: Her obstacle is _____.

Solutions:

a. She can _____.

b. Her mother can _____.

2. **Goal:** Lam wants to _____.

Obstacle: His obstacle is _____.

Solutions:

a. His grandchildren can _____.

b. His grandchildren can _____.

G Read how to use *when* to talk about goals.

1. *When* Bolin *graduates*, he *will* apply for a new position at work.

This sentence means: *First*, he will graduate. *Then* he will apply for a new position at work.

2. *When* his parents *come* to the United States, he *will* buy a house.

This sentence means: *First*, his parents will come to the United States. *Then* he will buy a house.

H Study the chart.

Future Time Clauses with *When*			
When + Subject	Verb (present)	Subject + *Will*	Base Verb
When Bolin	graduates,	he will	**apply** for a new position at work.*
When his parents	come to the United States,	he will	**buy** a house.
*Note: Place a comma after the *when* clause when it begins the sentence. The order of the clauses does not matter. You can also say, *Bolin will apply for a new position at work when he graduates.*			

I Complete the sentences below with your own ideas.

1. When Bolin's parents come to the United States, _his house will be too small_____.

2. When _____, they will buy a bigger house.

3. When Bolin's mother comes to stay, _____.

4. When _____, his boss will promote him.

5. When Bolin gets a better job, _____.

J CLASSIFY Bolin has a *personal* goal (buy a new home), an *educational* goal (graduate from college), and a *professional* goal (get a new position at work). What are your goals? Write them in the table below.

Personal	Educational	Professional
1. _____	1. _____	1. _____
2. _____	2. _____	2. _____
3. _____	3. _____	3. _____

K In groups, discuss your goals for the future.

EXAMPLE: When I graduate, I will get a new job.

L APPLY Write your goals on a separate piece of paper. Hang it up in a place where you can read your goals each day.

The Future

GOAL ▶ Write about a personal goal

A **Complete the paragraph below with *obstacles and solutions*.**

In the previous lesson, you wrote about your goals. Goals are things you want to achieve. Sometimes, we can have problems achieving them. These problems are called _____. When we figure out how to solve these problems, we have _____.

B **ANALYZE** **Choose one of the goals you wrote in the table in Lesson 2. Think of one obstacle to reaching your goal and two possible solutions.**

Goal: _____

Obstacle: _____

Solutions:

1. _____

_____

_____

2. _____

_____

_____

C **Share your ideas with a partner. Can your partner suggest other solutions?**

D **What is a paragraph? Discuss the following terms with your teacher.**

- A *paragraph* is a group of sentences about the same topic.
- A *topic sentence* is usually the first sentence in a paragraph. It introduces the topic or *main idea*.
- *Support sentences* are the sentences that follow the topic sentence. They give *details* about the topic.
- A *conclusion sentence* is the final sentence of the paragraph. It gives a *summary* of the paragraph.

E **Read the paragraph Tuba wrote about her goal.**

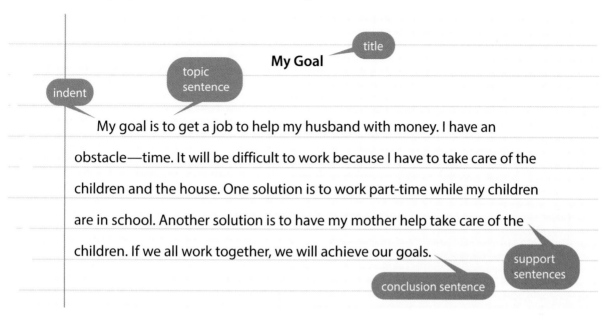

title

My Goal

topic sentence

indent

My goal is to get a job to help my husband with money. I have an

obstacle—time. It will be difficult to work because I have to take care of the

children and the house. One solution is to work part-time while my children

are in school. Another solution is to have my mother help take care of the

children. If we all work together, we will achieve our goals.

support sentences

conclusion sentence

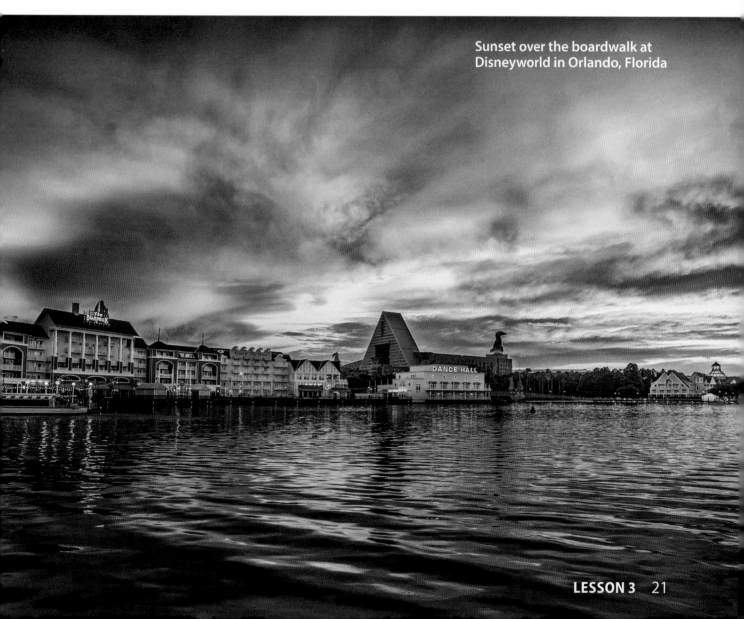

Sunset over the boardwalk at Disneyworld in Orlando, Florida

F ANALYZE Look again at Tuba's paragraph in **E** and answer the questions. Then write ideas for your own paragraph about the goal you chose in **B**.

1. What is Tuba's topic sentence?

_____

_____

_____

_____

1. Write your topic sentence.

_____

_____

_____

_____

_____

2. Tuba's support sentences are about her obstacle and her two possible solutions. What are her support sentences?

_____

_____

_____

_____

_____

_____

2. Write your three support sentences.

a. _____

_____

_____

b. _____

_____

_____

c. _____

_____

_____

3. What is Tuba's conclusion sentence?

_____

_____

_____

_____

3. Write your conclusion sentence.

_____

_____

_____

_____

G On a separate piece of paper, write a paragraph about your goal using correct paragraph formatting.

LESSON
4

Study Habits
GOAL ▶ Analyze study habits

A Answer the following questions. Then compare answers with a partner.

1. Where do you like to study?

_____

2. When do you usually study?

_____

3. How long do you study for?

_____

4. Do you listen to music when you study? Why or why not?

_____

_____

B **COMPARE** Look at the first picture. What is Luisa doing? Do you think she is learning anything? Why or why not? Look at the second picture. What is Michel doing? Is he learning anything? Discuss your ideas with a partner.

C Listen to the information about study habits and take notes. What are good and bad study habits? 🎧

_____

_____

_____

_____

D Read about study habits below.

      Good study habits can be very *beneficial* to you and your education. On the other hand, bad study habits can be *harmful* to your educational goals. First, let's talk about bad study habits.

      Many people have very busy schedules, and it is difficult for them to find time to study. One bad study habit is not studying before class. Another bad study habit is studying with *distractions* around, such as television, people talking, or loud music. A third bad habit is copying a friend's homework. These are just a few bad study habits, but you can easily change them into good study habits.

      There are many ways that you can *improve* your study habits. First, try to study at the same time every day. Do not make appointments at this time. This is your special study time. Second, find a good place to study, a place that is quiet and comfortable, so you can *concentrate*. Finally, do your homework on your own. Afterwards, you can find a friend to help you *go over* your work and check your answers.

E INTERPRET According to the reading, what are some bad study habits? Add one more idea.

not studying before class
_____

_____

_____

_____

F INTERPRET According to the reading, what are some good study habits? Add one more idea.

studying at the same time every day
_____

_____

_____

_____

_____

G Match each word or phrase with its correct definition. Write the letter.

1. _____ beneficial   a. bad for you

2. _____ harmful   b. get better

3. _____ distractions   c. review or check again

4. __b__ improve   d. good for you

5. _____ concentrate   e. think hard about something

6. _____ go over   f. things that disturb your studying

H Fill in the blanks with a word or phrase from **G**.

1. My English will _____ if I practice every day.

2. Please be quiet. I can't _____ on my homework.

3. Studying with a friend can be _____ because you can help each other.

4. When you finish taking a test, _____ your answers again.

5. It's hard to study when there are _____. Turn off the TV!

6. Bad study habits can be _____ to your educational goals.

I Choose three words or phrases from **G** and write sentences about your study habits on a separate piece of paper. Share your sentences with a partner.

J Think about your study habits. Fill in the table below.

Good Study Habits	Bad Study Habits
1.	1.
2.	2.
3.	3.

K COMPARE Share your answers with a partner. Which study habits are the same? Which study habits are different? Do you agree with these opinions?

Time Management

GOAL ▶ Manage time

A Read about Lara's problem. 🎧

Lara doesn't spend enough time with her family. The pie chart shows how Lara spends her time. She rarely has any free time to relax. Lara wants to find a way to balance her time, so she has decided to attend a lecture at school to learn better time-management strategies.

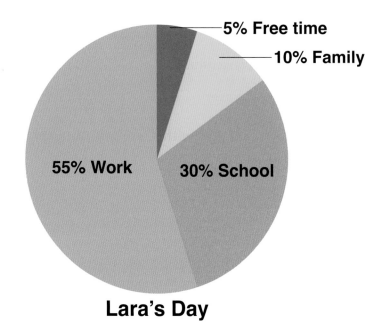

5% Free time
10% Family
55% Work
30% School

Lara's Day

B Answer the questions about Lara.

1. What is Lara's goal?

_____

2. What is her obstacle?

_____

3. What is her solution?

_____

C Listen to the lecture about time management. Listen for the main ideas. Do you agree? 🎧

Commuters deal with traffic while crossing 42nd Street in New York City.

D **DISCUSS** When you listen to a lecture, you can use an outline to help record important information. Look at the outline below and discuss it with your teacher.

1. Why is time management important?

   a. You stay organized.

   b. You accomplish everything that needs to get done.

   c. You _____.

2. How do you keep a schedule?

   a. Write down everything you need to do in a week.

   b. Put each task in a time slot.

   c. _____.

   d. Check off things that have been completed.

3. How can you add more time to your day?

   a. You can wake up earlier.

   b. You can ask _____.

   c. You can try doing _____ tasks at once.

4. What are other important things to consider about time management?

   a. Remember the important people in your life.

   b. _____.

   c. You are the boss of your schedule.

5. What are the benefits of managing your time?

   a. You will have more time.

   b. You will feel less _____.

   c. You will have time to _____.

   d. You will feel better about yourself.

E Listen to the lecture on time management again and complete the outline in D.

F A pie chart is a circle that is divided up into parts that equal 100%. Look at the pie chart, fill in the percentages below, and add them up. Do they equal 100%?

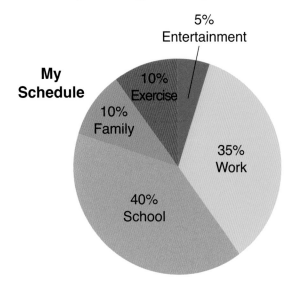

5%
Entertainment

My Schedule

10% Exercise

10% Family

35% Work

40% School

Work:	_____%
School:	_____%
Family:	_____%
Exercise:	_____%
Entertainment:	_____%
TOTAL	_____%

G On a separate piece of paper, create a pie chart to show how you spend your time. Make sure your chart equals 100%!

H REFLECT Answer the following questions about your own time-management strategies.

1. What problems do you have with time?

   I work ten hours a day, and I don't have time to study.

   _____

2. How could you add more time to your day? (Think about what you learned from the lecture.)

   _____

   _____

3. What are some time-management skills you learned that you would like to use in your life?

   _____

   _____

Explore the Workforce

GOAL ▶ Learn about character traits important for work

A **Discuss the following in a small group.**

1. Do you work? If so, what is your job?

2. Do you work full-time or part-time?

3. Are you happy with your job or would you like a different job?

4. What is the difference between a job and a career?

JOB:

when a person performs tasks in exchange for payment

CAREER:

a choice which results in a person learning skills and getting experience in a particular industry to earn money

B **INTERPRET** **There are sixteen career clusters recognized in the US. Here is a graphic showing six main fields and the corresponding career clusters. Read the infographic. What field do you think jobs 1–4 belong in?**

1. architect

   a. government and public administration

   b. finance

   c. industrial and engineering technology

2. nurse

   a. human services

   b. health services

   c. education and training

3. farmer

   a. natural resources and agriculture

   b. finance

   c. manufacturing

4. musician

   a. marketing

   b. arts and communication

   c. human services

Health Services
Therapeutic Services, Diagnostic Services, Health Information

Industrial & Engineering Technology
Manufacturing Production, Transportation Operation, Engineering and Technology, Construction

Arts & Communication
Audio and Video Technology, Printing Technology, Performing Arts

Human Services
Early Childhood and Development Services, Restaurants and Food Services, Public Management and Administration

Natural Resources & Agriculture
Food Products and Processing Systems, Agribusiness Systems, Animal Systems

Business, Management & Technology
Information Technology, Business Management and Administration, Marketing

C As a class, discuss the career clusters and jobs listed below. Write the job next to the career cluster.

~~food server~~	airplane mechanic	computer programmer	film editor
cable TV installer	appliance repair person	park ranger	artist
technical support representative		hotel housekeeper	

Career Cluster	Example Jobs
Hospitality and Tourism	Food server
Manufacturing	
Arts, A/V Technology and Communications	
Information Technology	

D Add one or two more jobs to each career cluster.

E REFLECT Circle the character traits that describe you.

ambitious	detail-oriented	honest	organized	reserved
calm	friendly	independent	outgoing	responsible
creative	hard-working	motivated	reliable	tech-savvy

F Think about what character traits are needed to do different jobs. For example, if you are a food server, you might be good with people, outgoing, organized, compassionate. Can you think of other character traits that a food server might have?

CHARACTER TRAITS: words that describe the qualities that make you who you are

Choose two of the jobs from above and write down the character traits needed to perform them.

Job	Character Traits Needed

G **SKIM** **Read the job advertisement quickly. Then answer the questions.**

Penelope's Garden is looking for an individual to join our team. Our ideal candidate is self-driven, motivated, trustworthy, punctual, and reliable.

Responsibilities

- Welcome and greet customers as they enter the store.
- Offer help and provide direct assistance to customers.
- Answer customer questions and concerns.
- Process purchases, returns, and exchanges.
- Handle customer complaints in a calm and professional manner.
- Report anything unusual or any major incidents to management.
- Organize and replenish front stock and help merchandise store.
- Maintain a clean and tidy work and retail space.
- Be enthusiastic and informative about all products.
- Take direction from and report to assigned supervisor.

Qualifications

- Friendly and outgoing personality
- Excellent verbal skills
- Experience in a florist shop or specialty sales experience; Computer skills
- Able to problem solve as issues arise

Available shifts and compensation: We have available shifts all days of the week. Compensation is $15.00 - $18.00/hour.

1. What do you think Penelope's Garden is? _____

2. What does this job pay? _____

3. Do you have to use a computer? _____

4. If you are organized, is this a good job for you? _____

_____

5. If you like to work by yourself, is this a good job for you? _____

_____

H **REFLECT** **Would this job be a good fit for you? Why or why not?**

I **Go online and find a job that fits your character traits.**

Review

A Exchange books with a partner. Have your partner complete the schedule.

	Monday	Tuesday	Wednesday	Thursday	Friday	Saturday	Sunday
Morning							
Afternoon							
Evening							

B Write sentences about your partner's schedule using the frequency adverbs.

1. (always) _____

2. (usually) _____

3. (often) _____

4. (sometimes) _____

5. (rarely) _____

6. (never) _____

C Now share your sentences with your partner and see if he or she agrees. Use the conversation below as a model.

Student A: You always work in the evenings.

Student B: Yes, I do.

D Complete the sentences with the correct verb form.

1. When Jason _____ (get) a better job, he

   _____ (buy) a new house.

2. Lilia _____ (join) her sister at college when

   she _____ (finish) her ESL class.

3. We _____ (run) a marathon when we _____

   (complete) our training program.

4. When Maria _____ (get) her bachelor's degree, she

   _____ (ask) her boss for a raise.

Learner Log	I can analyze and create schedules.
	☐ Yes ☐ No ☐ Maybe

E What are your goals for the future? Write sentences about your future goals using *when*.

1. When I finish this course, I will take the GED exam.

2. _____

3. _____

4. _____

5. _____

F Think of one obstacle and one solution for each goal you wrote in **E**. Complete the chart.

	Goal	Obstacle	Solution
2.			
3.			
4.			
5.			

G Match each word or phrase to its correct meaning. Draw a line.

_____ 1. paragraph   a. introduces your topic, or main idea

_____ 2. topic sentence   b. give details about your topic

_____ 3. support sentences   c. gives a summary of everything you wrote

_____ 4. conclusion sentence   d. a group of sentences about the same topic

Learner Log   I can identify goals and obstacles and suggest solutions.   I can write about a personal goal.
　　　　　　　　　　☐ Yes ☐ No ☐ Maybe　　　　　　　　　　　　☐ Yes ☐ No ☐ Maybe

Review

H Read the following sentences that make up a paragraph. Label each as a *topic* sentence (T), a *support* sentence (S), or a *conclusion* sentence (C). Remember, there can only be one topic sentence and one conclusion sentence.

1. I will buy books to study with and I will study very hard. _____

2. Within the next two years, I hope to have my license. _____

3. When I'm ready, I will register for the test. _____

4. My goal for the future is to get my real estate license. _____

5. When I am close to taking the test, I will ask my friend to help me. _____

I On a separate piece of paper, rewrite the sentences above in the correct order using correct paragraph formatting. Write a title for the paragraph.

J Write two good study habits.

1. _____

2. _____

K Write two good time-management strategies.

1. _____

2. _____

L Write the correct word or phrase from the box for each definition.

beneficial	concentrate	distractions	go over
goal	harmful	improve	obstacle

1. bad for you _____

2. get better at something _____

3. good for you _____

4. think hard about something _____

5. something you want to achieve _____

6. a problem _____

7. review something or check it again _____

8. things that bother you when you are studying _____

Learner Log	I can analyze study habits.	I can manage time.
	☐ Yes ☐ No ☐ Maybe	☐ Yes ☐ No ☐ Maybe

Make a Schedule

SOFT SKILL ▶ Collaboration

With a team, you will design a weekly schedule that includes your class and study time. You will identify good study habits and time-management strategies.

1. Form a team of four or five students. Choose a position for each member of your team.

Position	Job Description	Student Name
Student 1: Leader	Check that everyone speaks English and participates.	
Student 2: Secretary	Take notes on study habits and time-management strategies.	
Student 3: Designer	Design a weekly schedule.	
Students 4/5: Assistants	Help the secretary and the designer with their work.	

2. Design a weekly schedule. On your schedule, write in the days and times you have English class.

3. Decide on a goal that is related to learning English. Then think of one obstacle to your goal and two solutions.

COLLABORATION:
Sharing Ideas

As a team, you need to decide on a goal. Think of ways to let everyone express their ideas so that everyone is heard.

1. Go around in a circle and have each person say their idea. Then discuss and vote.

2. Have each person write their idea on a piece of paper. Have one person read the papers aloud and then vote.

Young people using computers to study or do research in a public library

4. Make a list of good study habits and a list of time-management strategies you would like to use.

5. Make a poster with all of the information from above: weekly schedule, goal, obstacle, solutions, good study habits, and time-management strategies.

6. Present your poster to the class.

Reading Challenge

A **PREDICT** Answer the questions before you read.

1. What is a "Dreamer"?

2. What do you think Areli's profession is?

3. What are illustrations?

4. Have you heard of the Dream Act or DACA? If so, what do you know?

B **Read about Areli Morales.**

C **ANALYZE** Find the correct answer.

1. What line talks about Areli's obstacle?

   a. line 3   b. line 7–8   c. line 12   d. line 18

2. In what line do we learn about the solution to her obstacle?

   a. line 3   b. line 9   c. line 12   d. line 18

3. Where do we see that she realized her goal?

   a. line 3   b. line 9   c. line 12   d. line 15–16

D **Look at the photo of the monarch butterflies. What do you think they symbolize?**

E **Monarch butterflies migrate every year, travel long distances, and face many obstacles. What are some of the obstacles that migrants face?**

F **REFLECT** Think about your life so far. Do you have a story similar to Areli's? Write it in your notebook and share it with a partner.

A Dreamer

Areli is a Dreamer. She was born in Puebla, Mexico. She lived there with her grandmother and cousins because her parents had moved to the United States to get better jobs and provide for their family. Areli was confused. She didn't want to leave her grandmother's house and move away from everything she knew. But she hated being away from her parents.

5   Eventually, Areli's parents were able to bring her to live with them in New York. At first, she didn't like New York. It was loud and busy and fast. She couldn't speak English and the kids at school teased her. They called her illegal because she wasn't a US citizen. She was worried that she could be sent back to Mexico.

But finally, the US began to feel like home to Areli. She realized that America is the land
10 of opportunity. On June 15, 2012, President Barack Obama announced a temporary program called DACA, allowing Dreamers to come forward, pass a background check, and apply for work permits. Areli's DACA was approved and she finally felt like she could pursue her dreams.

She attended and graduated from CUNY Brooklyn College with a bachelor's degree in childhood bilingual education and is currently a substitute elementary school teacher. She
15 wanted to tell her story to other immigrant children and in 2021, she published a children's book called *Areli is a Dreamer*. She hopes that her book will help children understand what people like her go through to realize their American dream.

Every autumn monarch butterflies migrate to Mexico to spend the winter.

2 Consumer Smarts

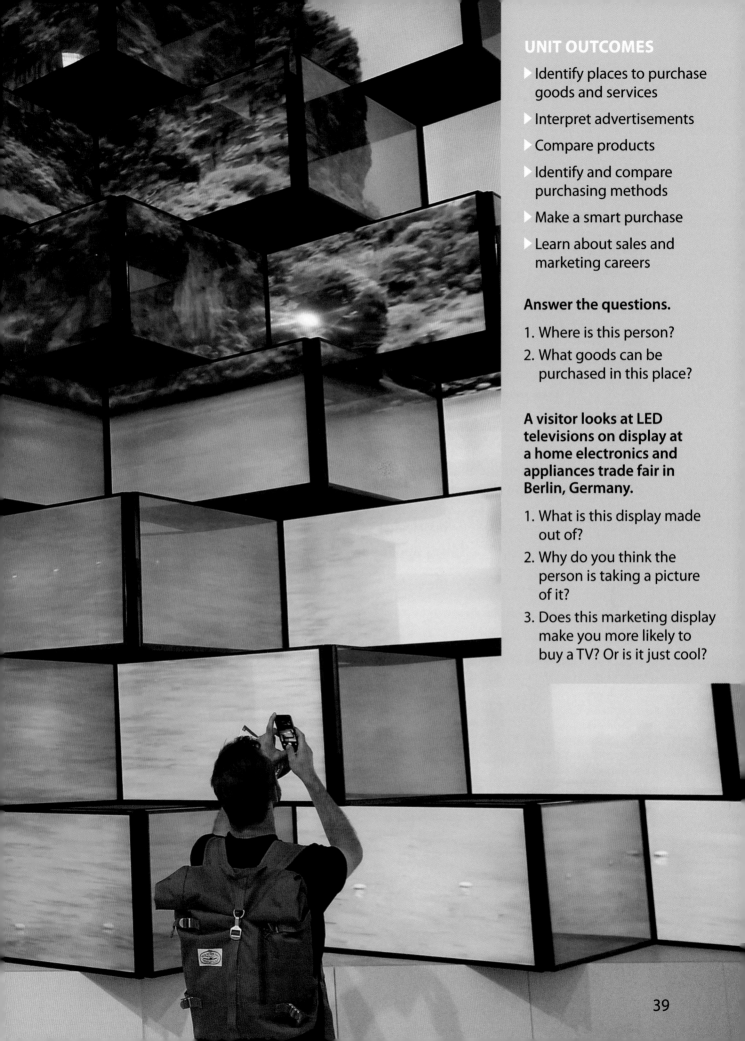

UNIT OUTCOMES

▶ Identify places to purchase goods and services

▶ Interpret advertisements

▶ Compare products

▶ Identify and compare purchasing methods

▶ Make a smart purchase

▶ Learn about sales and marketing careers

Answer the questions.

1. Where is this person?

2. What goods can be purchased in this place?

A visitor looks at LED televisions on display at a home electronics and appliances trade fair in Berlin, Germany.

1. What is this display made out of?

2. Why do you think the person is taking a picture of it?

3. Does this marketing display make you more likely to buy a TV? Or is it just cool?

39

Shopping for Goods and Services

GOAL ▶ Identify places to purchase goods and services

A **Look at the photos. What goods or services can you purchase at these places?**

B **CLASSIFY** **Which of the places below sell goods and which sell services? Which sell both? Complete the diagram.**

bank	dry cleaner	hair salon	pharmacy
car wash	gas station	jewelry store	~~post office~~
department store	~~grocery store~~	~~laundromat~~	tailor

Sell goods

grocery store

_____

_____

_____

_____

_____

Sell services

laundromat

_____

_____

_____

_____

post office

_____

_____

_____

C **EXPLAIN** Where can you purchase each of the following items? Write the places. Some items may have more than one answer. Check (✓) if this is an item you could / would buy online.

1. medicine   _____pharmacy_____   yes ☐   no ☐

2. a table   _____   yes ☐   no ☐

3. a notebook   _____   yes ☐   no ☐

4. a bracelet   _____   yes ☐   no ☐

5. boots   _____   yes ☐   no ☐

6. a refrigerator   _____   yes ☐   no ☐

7. bread   _____   yes ☐   no ☐

8. motor oil   _____   yes ☐   no ☐

9. a shirt   _____   yes ☐   no ☐

10. stamps   _____   yes ☐   no ☐

D We use the expression to *get something done* when we talk about services we purchase. Study the chart with your teacher.

To Get Something Done				
Subject	*Get*	**Object**	**Past Participle**	**Example Sentence**
I	get	my hair	cut.	I get my hair cut every month. (present)
She	got	her clothes	cleaned.	She got her clothes cleaned yesterday. (past)

Two entrepreneurs set up a dry cleaner where people can get their clothes cleaned.

E **Where can you receive the following services?**

1. get your hair cut   _____ hair salon _____

2. get your checks cashed   _____

3. get your clothes repaired   _____

4. get your car washed   _____

5. get your car fixed   _____

6. get your clothes washed   _____

F **Answer the following questions in complete sentences. Listen and check your answers.** 🎧

1. Where do you get your hair cut?
   _I get my hair cut at the hair salon._____

2. Where did you get your prescription filled?
   _____

3. Where do you get your packages mailed?
   _____

4. Where did you get your keys made?
   _____

5. Where did you get your gas tank filled up?
   _____

6. Where do you get your clothes washed?
   _____

G **APPLY** **Imagine you are new to the neighborhood. Ask your partner questions about places in the area.**

EXAMPLE: **Student A:**   Where can I get my car washed?
               Student B: You can get your car washed at the car wash on Maple Street.

H **Think of a shopping center near your school or home. Go online and see what stores the shopping center has. Make a list to share with your class.**

_____

_____

_____

_____

Advertisements

GOAL ▶ Interpret advertisements

A FIND OUT Discuss the following questions with your classmates.

1. What are advertisements? Where can you find them?

2. What information can you find in advertisements?

Life ONLINE

It's important to see some things in person before buying, but to get the best price, consider purchasing online. Google's shopping filter will compare prices from different vendors. You can also add a coupon extension to your browsers that will automatically check all available discounts for a product before you check out.

B Read the advertisements.

1.

SAVE ON AN OIL CHANGE AT BOB'S AUTO SERVICE

Most cars now only $59.95. Includes up to five quarts of oil, new oil filter, and labor.

Offer expires August 5th

CLICK HERE FOR AN ESTIMATE

2.

FUN FOR THE ENTIRE FAMILY WITH THE NEW ENERX SYSTEM

Stream movies and live TV, listen to music, AND play games with this all-in-one system.

Register now for free installation

CLICK HERE

3.

MUSIC FACTORY OUTLET SALE

CLICK HERE

Top of the line earbuds starting at $79. Noise cancelling headphones starting from $110.

30%-70% off original prices of well-known name brands.

$10 discount with code: STEREO10.

4.

BIKE SALE
AT WHEEL WORLD

SAVE 25%
Regular priced bikes at $299 now on sale for $249. All bikes come with a one-year warranty.

▶ CLICK HERE TO VISIT OUR SITE

C **INTERPRET** Read the ads. Find the word or phrase in the box. Match each with the correct meaning.

warranty   installation   ~~lowest price available~~   free   everything included   expire

1. starting from ___lowest price available___   2. guarantee _____

3. no charge _____   4. to come to an end _____

5. all in one _____   6. to set up for use _____

D Read the ads again and choose the correct answers.

1. What does the oil change NOT include?

   ☐ oil   ☐ oil filter   ☐ windshield wiper fluid

2. When does the offer expire for the oil change?

   ☐ May 8th   ☐ August 8th   ☐ August 5th

3. What does the entertainment system not include?

   ☐ live TV   ☐ music   ☐ speakers

4. How much is the entertainment system?

   ☐ $150   ☐ $79.95   ☐ It doesn't say.

5. According to the ad, who is the entertainment system good for?

   ☐ dads   ☐ kids   ☐ the entire family

6. What is for sale at the Music Factory outlet?

   ☐ earbuds only   ☐ headphones only   ☐ earbuds and headphones

7. What is the discount at Music Outlet?

   ☐ $79   ☐ $110   ☐ 30-70%

8. What is the regular price of the bikes?

   ☐ $150.00   ☐ $299.00   ☐ $250.00

9. How much are the bikes discounted?

   ☐ $25   ☐ 25%   ☐ $37.00

10. Which item(s) come with a warranty?

   ☐ entertainment systems   ☐ bicycles   ☐ entertainment systems and bicycles

E **REFLECT** Which product do you like the best? Why?

_____

_____

F Read the two ads and complete the table.

Cleaning Services		
Company	Happy Helpers	Kate's Cleaners
Phone Number		
Product or Service		
Price		
Discounts		
Other Information		

G JUSTIFY Which cleaning service would you choose? Why?

_____

_____

H Choose a product or service you want to sell. On a separate piece of paper, create a similar chart to the one in **F** and complete it.

I APPLY Find some online ads. What special offers do they include?

Making Comparisons

GOAL ▶ Compare products

A **IDENTIFY** Label the different parts of the laptop. Write the numbers.

1. headphones jack	2. power cable socket	3. power cable	4. touchpad
5. keyboard	6. display	7. camera	

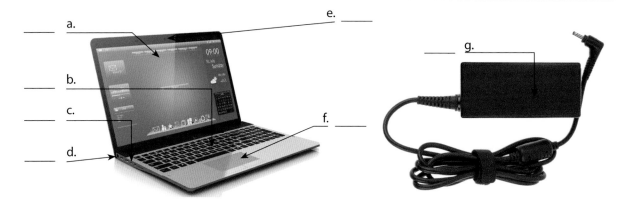

B **What should you look for when you buy a laptop? Point to the adjectives.**

Weight:	Is the computer heavy or light?	**Price:**	Is the computer expensive or cheap?
Display:	Is the screen large or small?	**Hard Drive:**	Is the hard drive big or small?
Memory:	How much memory does the computer have?		

C **DESCRIBE** Use the adjectives from B to talk about the laptops in the table.

EXAMPLE: The JCN laptop has a large display.

	JCN	Doshiba	Vintel	Shepland	Kontaq
Price	$1,310	$248	$695	$1,350	$469
Display size	17.3″	14″	14″	13.5″	15.6″
Weight	5.6 lbs	3.96 lbs	3.52 lbs	3.06 lbs	3.75 lbs
Memory	16GB	4GB	12GB	16GB	8GB
Hard drive	512GB	64GB	256GB	512GB	128GB
Battery life	10 hours	14 hours	10 hours	17 hours	5.5 hours
Touchscreen	No	No	Yes	Yes	No

D Study the chart with your classmates and teacher.

Comparatives				
	Adjective	**Comparative**	**Rule**	**Example Sentence**
Short Adjectives	cheap	cheap**er**	Add -*er* to the end of the adjective.	Your computer was *cheaper* than my computer.
Long Adjectives	expensive	**more** expensive	Add *more* before the adjective.	The new computer was *more expensive* than the old one.
Irregular Adjectives	good, bad	**better, worse**	These adjectives are irregular.	The computer at school is *better* than this one.
Remember to use *than* after a comparative adjective followed by a noun.				

E Use the rules in **D** and the spelling rules to make comparative adjectives.

1. slow   _____slower_____   2. small   _____

3. wide   _____   4. big   _____

5. heavy   _____   6. fast   _____

7. beautiful _____   8. interesting _____

Spelling Rules

hot	→	**hotter**
easy	→	**easier**
large	→	**larger**
pretty	→	**prettier**

F Make comparative sentences about the laptops in **C**. Listen and check your answers. 🎧

1. The Kontaq / expensive / Vintel

_____

2. The JCN's battery life / long / the Kontaq's battery life

_____

3. The Doshiba / heavy / the Vintel

_____

4. The JCN's hard drive / big / the Kontaq's hard drive

_____

G **EVALUATE** Talk to your partner. Which laptop in **C** would you buy? Using comparatives, give three reasons for your choice.

H Study the chart with your teacher.

Superlatives				
	Adjective	**Superlative**	**Rule**	**Example Sentence**
Short Adjectives	cheap	**the** cheap**est**	Add *the* before and *-est* to the end of the adjective.	Your computer is **the cheapest**.
Long Adjectives	expensive	**the most** expensive	Add *the most* before the adjective.	He bought **the most expensive** computer in the store.
Irregular Adjectives	good, bad	**the best, the worst**	These adjectives are irregular.	The computers at school are **the best**.
Always use *the* before a superlative.				

I Use the rules in **H** and the spelling rules to make superlative adjectives.

1. slow _____the slowest_____

2. small _____

3. wide _____

4. big _____

5. heavy _____

6. fast _____

7. beautiful _____

8. interesting _____

Spelling Rules

hot → **the hottest**

easy → **the easiest**

large → **the largest**

pretty → **the prettiest**

J Make superlative sentences about the laptops in **C**.

1. large _____The JCN laptop has the largest display._____

2. expensive _____

3. cheap _____

4. light _____

5. long battery life _____

6. small hard drive _____

K APPLY Write six questions about the laptops in **C** using comparatives and superlatives in your notebook. Ask your classmates to answer your questions. Then discuss which laptop you would get. Remember to discuss what you would use it for. Is it for web browsing, email, games, or for editing photos? Don't forget to think about the accessories you will need.

EXAMPLE: Which laptop is faster, the JCN or the Vintel?

_____

_____

Cash or Charge?

GOAL ▶ Identify and compare purchasing methods

A IDENTIFY Terron uses four different ways to make purchases. What are they?

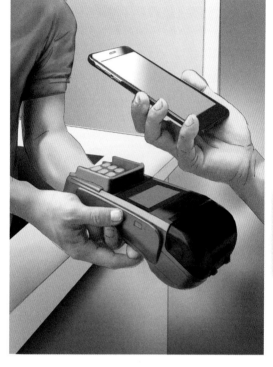

GOLD CARD
CREDIT CARD
1234 3450 1234 5678
05/25
Terron A. Kabiro

Streetview Bank
DEBIT CARD
5634 5678 1234 5678
02/25
Terron A. Kabiro

B Write the correct word next to its description. You will use some of the items twice.

cash	credit card	debit card	online payment	personal check

1. This is a written request to your bank asking them to pay money out of your account.

   _____

2. This allows you to borrow money to make purchases. _____

3. Coins and bills are this. _____

4. This allows a store to take money directly from your account to pay for purchases.

   _____

5. This allows you to buy now and pay later. _____

6. You can get cash out of the ATM with this. _____

7. You can use your phone to do this. _____

C **COMPARE** Talk about the advantages and disadvantages of each purchasing method. Use the conversation below as a model. Then complete the table.

Life
ONLINE

What are the benefits of making online payments? The money can arrive quickly. You don't have to pay for a stamp. It is more secure (your mail could get stolen). Can you think of some other benefits?

Student A: Cash is good because it is quick and easy.

Student B: Yes, but if you lose cash, you cannot replace it.

	Cash	Credit Card	Debit Card	Personal Check
Advantages	quick and easy			
Disadvantages	can't replace			

D Talk to a partner about the purchasing method you prefer and why.

E Listen to Terron and his wife, Leilani, talk about purchasing methods. Make a list of the things they say they *have* to do and *must* do.

Have to	*Must*

F We use *must* and *have to* when something is necessary. *Must* is a little stronger than *have* to. Study the chart below with your teacher.

Must vs. Have to			
Subject	**Modal**	**Base Verb**	**Example Sentence**
I / You / We / They	have to must	save pay off	I **have to** save money for a vacation. I **must** pay off my credit card every month.
He / She / It	has to must	keep	She **has to** keep track of her money. He **must** keep track of his money.

G Complete each statement with the correct form of *must* or *have to* and a verb from the box.

check	keep	make	pay	put

1. You _____must_____ _____pay_____ your bills if you want a good credit history.

2. You _____ _____ your cash in a safe place.

3. You _____ _____ track of the online payments you make.

4. You _____ _____ the minimum amount on your credit card every month.

5. You _____ _____ sure you have enough money in the bank when you write a personal check.

6. You _____ _____ your balance before you get cash out of an ATM.

H **APPLY** Choose one purchasing method and write a paragraph in your notebook on why you think it is better than the rest. Use one of the topic sentences below to get you started. Use comparative and superlative adjectives.

Topic Sentence 1: The best purchasing method is always cash.

Topic Sentence 2: I use a debit card to make purchases.

Topic Sentence 3: Personal checks are the best way to purchase items.

Topic Sentence 4: In my opinion, you should always use credit cards to make purchases.

Topic Sentence 5: Online payments make life easier.

Think before You Buy

GOAL ▶ Make a smart purchase

A Read about making smart purchases.

You make a smart purchase when you think and plan before you buy something. First of all, you make a decision to buy something. This is the easy part. The second step is comparison shopping. You comparison shop by reading advertisements, going to different stores, and talking to friends and family. Third, you choose which product you are going to buy.

Do you have enough money to buy this product? If you don't, the next step is to start saving. This may take a while depending on how much you need to save. Once you have enough money, you are ready to make your purchase. If you follow these steps to make a purchase, you will be a smart consumer. And smart consumers make smart purchases!

B **SEQUENCE** Order the steps from 1 to 5 according to the text above.

_____	make the purchase	_____	read advertisements
__1__	decide to buy something	_____	choose the best deal
_____	save money		

C Rewrite the steps in **B** after the words below.

First, *decide to buy something* _____.

Second, _____.

Next, _____.

Then, _____.

Finally, _____.

A busy day on Fifth Ave. in New York City

D *Sequencing transitions* are used to describe stages of a process. Study the examples in the box.

First, Fourth,	First of all, Next,	Second, Then,	Second of all, Lastly,	Third, Finally,

E Put the steps in the correct order.

You
Use *you* to talk about people in general.

_____ You decide to buy it.

_____ You find out the price.

__1__ You see something in a store you want to buy.

_____ You decide to use your credit card.

_____ You think about if you have enough money to pay for it or not.

_____ You pay for it.

_____ You think about if you want to pay cash or use your credit card.

F **APPLY** Add sequencing transitions to the steps above to write a paragraph about making a smart purchase.

_____

_____

_____

_____

_____

_____

_____

_____

_____

_____

_____

G APPLY Imagine you are going to buy a laptop. In groups, decide on a list of considerations to make a smart purchase.

1. _____
2. _____
3. _____
4. _____
5. _____
6. _____
7. _____
8. _____

H COMPOSE Write a paragraph about buying a laptop. Use sequencing transitions.

_____
_____
_____
_____
_____
_____

Having the right equipment helps with work and studying.

Explore the Workforce

GOAL ▶ Learn about sales and marketing careers

A **COMPARE** What is the difference between *Sales* and *Marketing*? Discuss with a group. Then read.

What is Marketing?	**What are Careers in Sales?**
Marketing is advertising, sales strategies, and media planning. These create brand awareness to sell a product or service. Marketing could be traditional, such as radio, television and billboard ads, or more modern strategies, such as internet ads and social media.	Careers in sales involve selling a product or service. Salespeople are good at promoting the best features of a product to the consumer. Both marketing and sales careers require people who understand the target audience and the consumer's decision-making process.

B **ANALYZE** Look at the chart. Which are the worst / best paid jobs?

Common Sales and Marketing Jobs	
JOB	**NATIONAL AVERAGE SALARY**
Retail Sales Associate	$25,251 / year
Telemarketer	$27,602 / year
Social Media Manager	$44,689 / year
Marketing Specialist	$50,818 / year
Copywriter	$55,648 / year
Sales Representative	$58,722 / year
Insurance Agent	$59,430 / year
Marketing Manager	$67,791 / year
Sales Manager	$76,022 / year
Product Manager	$106,415 year

Useful terms

brand: the name of the company with their logo is the "brand"

brand awareness: how familiar a consumer is with a brand or its products

consumer: the person buying the product or service

target audience: the specific type of person who will buy a product. For example, older people with hearing loss are the "target audience" for hearing aids.

C Discuss with a partner. What do you think the people in these jobs do?

EXAMPLE: I think an Insurance Agent sells insurance.

D What do you think a sales manager does? Listen and complete the job description below.

Job Description: _____ Sales Manager _____

Salary: _____

Duties: A sales manager is in charge of a _____ of sales associates and _____ them achieve their _____ _____. A sales manager finds, _____, and _____ new _____. Sales managers check on the _____ of their associates and _____ if they need it. They also _____ sales _____ and make sure the _____ are satisfied.

E What traits are needed to be a good sales manager? Circle the traits below.

motivated	reliable	organized	outgoing	friendly
detail-oriented	tech-savvy	calm	responsible	hard-working
independent	creative	reserved	honest	ambitious

F **REFLECT** Do you think you would be a good sales manager? Why or why not? Write a few sentences and then share with a partner.

_____

_____

_____

_____

G Review the different types of degrees in the Pre-Unit. Complete the chart.

Education	Number of Years to Complete
High School Diploma	4
Associate Degree	
Bachelor's Degree	
Master's Degree	

H INTERPRET Look at the pie chart below. What information can you find in the chart?

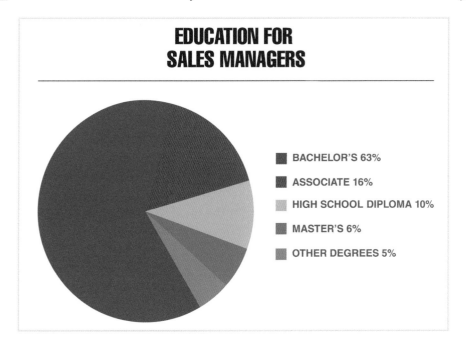

EDUCATION FOR
SALES MANAGERS

■ BACHELOR'S 63%

◩ ASSOCIATE 16%

▨ HIGH SCHOOL DIPLOMA 10%

▦ MASTER'S 6%

▨ OTHER DEGREES 5%

I Choose the correct answer.

1. _____ of sales managers have only a high school diploma.

   a. 63%   b. 16%   c. 10%   d. 6%

2. Many sales managers have a _____ .

   a. Bachelor's degree   b. Associate degree   c. Master's degree   d. high school diploma

3. You need to get a Master's degree to be a sales manager.

   a. True   b. False

4. _____ of sales managers have an Associate degree.

   a. 63%   b. 16%   c. 10%   d. 6%

J Go online and find a job advertisement for a sales manager. Answer the following questions.

1. What is the job title?

2. Where is the job?

3. Is it full-time or part-time?

4. What is the salary range?

5. What experience does the job need?

Review

A Where can you purchase the following goods or services? Write the places below.

1. shampoo _____
2. soccer ball _____
3. stamps _____
4. prescription refill _____
5. washing machine _____
6. fruit _____
7. clothes cleaned _____
8. shoes _____

B Write the present form of *get* and the past participle of the verb in parentheses.

1. He _____ *gets* _____ his car _____ *washed* _____ at the local car wash. (wash)

2. She _____ her hair _____ at the hair salon. (cut)

3. He _____ his car _____ at the automotive shop. (fix)

4. They _____ their clothes _____ at the dry cleaners. (clean)

C Read the ads from two car dealerships and answer the questions below.

Hill's Xonda
Xonda Pilot with all the bells and whistles

$36,999

Includes free gas for a year!

Xonda of Albilene
Fully loaded Xonda Pilot

$37,999

(includes tax, title, and license)

Come test drive your new car!
0% financing

1. Which car is cheaper? _____

2. What is good about the offer from Hill's? _____

3. What is good about the offer from Albilene? _____

4. Which dealership would you buy from? _____
   Why? _____

D Complete the following statements with a comparative or a superlative adjective. Use *than* where necessary.

1. My new watch was _____*cheaper than*_____ my old watch. (cheap)

2. This computer is _____ one in the store. (fast)

3. That mirror is _____ the one we have now. (tall)

4. This box is much _____ that one. What's in it? (heavy)

5. _____ paintings in the world are painted by that artist. (beautiful)

6. Do you think that the book is _____ the movie? (interesting)

7. I always pay by credit card. It's _____ way to pay. (easy)

8. My neighbor's house is _____ our house. (big)

9. Do you think this car is _____ the one you have? (good)

E Imagine that you are going to buy a new car—your dream car. Write sentences comparing your old car to your new car.

My new car is faster than my old car.

_____

_____

_____

_____

F What is the best restaurant in your neighborhood? Write sentences comparing this restaurant to all the other restaurants in the neighborhood.

Talk and Wok has the friendliest service in the neighborhood.

_____

_____

_____

_____

Learner Log   I can compare products.
☐ Yes ☐ No ☐ Maybe

G Write a sentence about each of the following purchasing methods. Use *must* or *have to*.

1. cashier's check: *You must be careful not to lose a cashier's check.*

2. cash: _____

3. personal check: _____

4. online payment: _____

5. credit card: _____

H Imagine that your friend is going to buy a new television. What steps would you tell him or her to take? Write them below.

1. _____

2. _____

3. _____

4. _____

5. _____

I Write a paragraph using the steps you wrote above. Use sequencing transitions.

_____

_____

_____

_____

J Choose four new words from this unit. Write each word and an example sentence on an index card. Study the words while you are traveling to school or eating your breakfast.

Learner Log	I can identify and compare purchasing methods.	I can make a smart purchase.
	Yes No Maybe	Yes No Maybe

Two Advertisements and a Purchase Plan

SOFT SKILL ▶ Presentation

1. Form a team of four or five students. Choose positions for each member of your team.

Position	Job Description	Student Name(s)
Student 1: **Team Leader**	Check that everyone speaks English. Check that everyone participates.	
Student 2: **Secretary**	Write the advertisement with help from the team. Take notes for the team.	
Student 3: **Designer**	Design an advertisement layout.	
Students 4/5: **Spokespeople**	Plan presentations.	

Part 1—Create Advertisements

1. Create two different advertisements for the same product or service.

2. Present your ads to the class and then display them in the classroom.

Part 2—Create a Purchase Plan

1. Take time to evaluate and choose a product or service to buy from all the ads on the wall.

2. Compare two of the ads, writing four comparative statements about why one is better than the other.

3. Choose one product or service to buy and write a purchase plan—the considerations needed to make a smart purchase.

4. Present your comparisons and purchase plan to the class.

Presentation:
Plan Your Presentation

Your presentation should be more than just reading from your notes. Each person should choose one part to present. Choose what is interesting to you, and find a way to make it interesting to your listeners.

Reading Challenge

A **PREDICT** Look at the company's logo in the photo. What do you think it is a picture of? What types of food and drink do you think they serve at this café?

B Match the vocabulary word to its correct meaning.

_____ 1. brunch   a. money that a person gets if he or she loses his or her job

_____ 2. pandemic   b. evidence that something is true

_____ 3. unemployment   c. a meal that combines breakfast and lunch

_____ 4. proof   d. a disease that happens to people all over the world

C Read the text.

D **SEQUENCE** Put the events in the correct order.

_____ Carolina collected unemployment.

___1___ Carolina lived in Guatemala City.

_____ Carolina lost her job.

_____ Carolina worked as a housekeeper.

_____ Carolina built her café.

_____ Carolina found a chef and business partner.

_____ Carolina crossed the border with her mother.

_____ Carolina opened Tikal Café.

E On a separate piece of paper, rewrite the sentences in **D** in the correct order, adding in extra details from the text. Sometimes, change the name Carolina to "she" to avoid too much repetition and add transitions like *such as*, *then*, *next*, etc.

EXAMPLE: Carolina lived in Guatemala City. In 2008, she came to the US with her mother. Then...

F **EXPAND** Imagine you are planning a visit to Brooklyn for brunch. What would you order?

Rising to the Challenge 🎧

Tikal Café is a brunch and coffee shop located in Brooklyn, New York. If you go to its website, you will see delicious menu items such as Avocado Toast, Winter Porridge, a Walnut Pesto Quesadilla and Coconut Yogurt. You can drink Matcha, Iced Lavender Lattes, or Cold Brew Coffee. But what you won't see on the website is that the café is owned by an immigrant,
5   Carolina Hernandez from Guatemala.

Carolina is from Guatemala City, Guatemala, and came to the US with her mother in 2008. For over 10 years, she worked two to three jobs so she could save up enough money to open her own business. Sometimes, she worked 18-hour days. She used the money from her housekeeping job to survive and pay her bills. And she used the money from her food serving
10 job to save for her dream.

Unfortunately, when the pandemic hit in 2020, she lost all of her jobs. She was able to collect unemployment, but she wasn't happy. Carolina was a hard worker and wanted to work to earn her money, not sit on the couch and watch Netflix. So, she found a business partner, who is now the chef at the café, and picked out a location close to her home. She started with
15 an empty space and eventually built Tikal Café, a neighborhood spot where locals can come to enjoy a cup of coffee and a delicious meal. From housekeeper to restaurant owner—Carolina is living proof of the American Dream.

Carolina Hernandez's hard work made her dream come true.

The Skinny House
(Spite House)

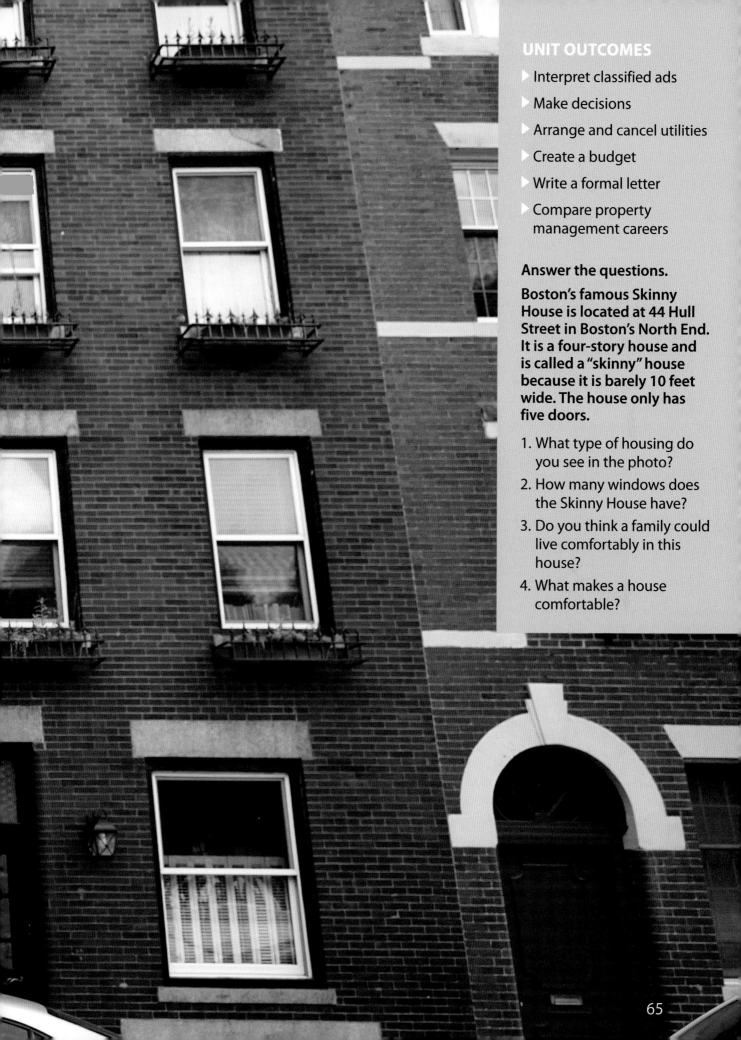

UNIT OUTCOMES

▶ Interpret classified ads

▶ Make decisions

▶ Arrange and cancel utilities

▶ Create a budget

▶ Write a formal letter

▶ Compare property management careers

Answer the questions.

Boston's famous Skinny House is located at 44 Hull Street in Boston's North End. It is a four-story house and is called a "skinny" house because it is barely 10 feet wide. The house only has five doors.

1. What type of housing do you see in the photo?

2. How many windows does the Skinny House have?

3. Do you think a family could live comfortably in this house?

4. What makes a house comfortable?

65

House Hunting

GOAL ▶ Interpret classified ads

A **EXPLAIN** Think about the place where you live. How did you find it? What are some different ways to find housing?

B Online classified ads and social media sites have housing information. Write the title of each ad. Then rank them in order from your favorite (1) to least favorite (6).

a. Sunny studio	d. Spacious four-bedroom
b. Sunny one-bedroom with high ceilings	e. Large apartment with garage and pool
c. ~~Two-bedroom in a gated community~~	f. Charming condo with balcony

1. _Two-bedroom in a gated community_
This clean two-bedroom has one bathroom, air conditioning, new appliances, and is near freeways. It is situated in a gated community. Gas, water, and trash collection are included. (Contact Agent)
Available August 1st. $1,495

2. _____
This sunny first-floor studio has a yard, stove, and a refrigerator. Cats are OK. The first and last month's rent and security deposit are required. $850 (Contact Agent)

3. _____
This spacious four-bedroom condo has a pool, a garage, a washer and dryer, and is close to local schools. No pets allowed. $3,000 (Contact Agent)

4. _____
This charming one-bedroom condo is in great condition. It has one bathroom, a carport, a large balcony, carpeting, and it's an easy walk to the town center. $1,300 (Contact Agent)

5. _____
This sunny, one-bedroom with a huge veranda has a one-car garage, a washer and dryer, high ceilings, and a security guard. $1,100 (Contact Agent)

6. _____
This large apartment has two floors, three bedrooms, two bathrooms, a garage, and a pool. $2,200 (Contact Agent)

C Work with a partner. Make a list of the housing vocabulary in **B** that is new to you. Discuss with your classmates and teacher.

D COMPARE Discuss the questions about the ads in **B** with your partner.

1. Which one-bedroom apartment has higher rent?

2. Look at ads 1 and 5. Which apartment has more bedrooms?

3. Look at ads 1 and 6. Which apartment has more bathrooms?

E Study the charts.

Comparatives Using Nouns	
Our new apartment has **more bedrooms** than our old one. Our old apartment had **fewer bedrooms** than our new one.	Use *more* or *fewer* to compare count nouns.
Rachel's apartment gets **more light** than Pablo's apartment. Pablo's apartment gets **less light** than Rachel's apartment.	Use *more* or *less* to compare noncount nouns.

Superlatives Using Nouns	
Rachel's apartment has **the most bedrooms**. Phuong's apartment has **the fewest bedrooms**.	Use *the most* or *the fewest* for count nouns.
Rachel's apartment has **the most light**. Phuong's apartment has **the least light**.	Use *the most* or *the least* for noncount nouns.

F Complete the sentences with *more* or *most*.

1. Kim's house has _____ bedrooms than Jen's house.

2. The Worshams' apartment gets the _____ light.

3. That condo has _____ appliances than this one.

4. Her house has the _____ rooms.

G Complete the sentences with *fewer*, *less*, *fewest*, or *least*.

1. John's house has _____ bathrooms than Brad's place.

2. The small condo has _____ light than the big one.

3. The small condo has the _____ space.

4. Their apartment has the _____ windows.

H SCAN Work with a partner. Scan the rental ads and ask and answer the questions. Answer in complete sentences.

a. This first-floor apartment has two bedrooms, 1.5 bathrooms, a garage, and a gym.
   Price: $1,275 per month **Security deposit:** $500 (Contact Agent)

b. This large five-bedroom, two-bathroom house with a two-car garage, washer / dryer hookups, and high ceilings is in a quiet neighborhood.
   Price: $3,200 per month **Security deposit:** $2,000 (Contact Agent)

c. This beautiful three-bedroom condo has three bathrooms, a garage for two cars, a large patio, and wood floors. It is located close to local shops.
   Price: $1,700 per month **Security deposit:** $600 (Contact Agent)

d. This bright, top-floor studio has a balcony and new appliances. Cats are OK. First and last month's rent are due at signing.
   Price: $1,000 per month **Security deposit:** $550 (Contact Agent)

1. Which place has more bathrooms: the house or the condo?

2. Which place has the most bedrooms?

3. Which place has the highest rent?

4. Which place has more bedrooms: the condo or the apartment?

5. Which place has the lowest security deposit?

Scan
Quickly look for the answers in a text without reading everything.

I Write sentences using comparatives and superlatives to compare the rentals in **H**.

1. The apartment has fewer bedrooms than the house. _____.

2. _____

3. _____

4. _____

5. _____

6. _____

J Search for classified housing ads online or on social media. Find an ad that you like and share your notes with the class.

Time to Move

GOAL ▶ Make decisions

A Read about the Nguyen family.

The Nguyen family lives in Cedarville, Texas. Vu Nguyen came from Vietnam twenty years ago and met his wife, Mariana, in Texas. The Nguyens have four children—two sons and two daughters. They are currently living in a two-bedroom apartment, which is too small for all six of them. They would like to stay in Cedarville, but they need a bigger place. Vu recently got a raise at work, so the Nguyen family wants to move.

B **INTERPRET** Listen to the Nguyen family talk about their housing preferences. Check the boxes next to the things they would like to have in their new apartment.

1. ☐ 2 bedrooms

2. ☐ 3 bedrooms

3. ☐ 2 bathrooms

4. ☐ 3 bathrooms

5. ☐ convenient location

6. ☐ tennis courts

7. ☐ pool

8. ☐ security guard

9. ☐ big windows

10. ☐ garage

11. ☐ yard

12. ☐ air-conditioning

13. ☐ carpeting

14. ☐ balcony

15. ☐ washer/dryer

C Compare your answers with a partner.

D Study the chart with your classmates and teacher.

Review: Yes / No Questions and Answers with Do				
Questions				**Short Answers**
Do	**Subject**	**Base Verb**	**Example Question**	
Do	I / you / we / they	have	Do they have a yard?	Yes, they do. / No, they don't.
Does	he / she / it	want	Does she want air conditioning?	Yes, she does. / No, she doesn't.

E Practice asking and answering *Yes / No* questions with a partner. Use the Nguyen family preferences in **B**.

Student A: Do they want <u>five bedrooms</u>?

Student B: No, they don't.

Yes/No **Questions** 🎧

Do they have a yard?

Do you want five bedrooms?

Does it have a balcony?

F **CONSTRUCT** Write *Yes / No* questions that you could ask the Nguyens.

1. <u>Do you want a bathtub?</u>

2. _____

3. _____

4. _____

5. _____

6. _____

G With a partner, practice asking and answering your questions.

H **VISUALIZE** Imagine you are going to buy or rent a new home. Write the number of bedrooms and bathrooms you want. Then check your preferences. Add other preferences that are not on the list.

_____ bedrooms

_____ bathrooms

☐ yard

☐ balcony

☐ pool

☐ washer / dryer

☐ air conditioning

☐ convenient location

☐ garage

☐ carport

☐ refrigerator

☐ _____

☐ _____

☐ _____

I Write five _Yes / No_ questions you can ask your partner about his or her housing preferences. Do not write the answers yet.

1. _Do you want a balcony?_ _____

Answer: _____

2. _____

Answer: _____

3. _____

Answer: _____

4. _____

Answer: _____

5. _____

Answer: _____

6. _____

Answer: _____

J Work with a partner. Ask and answer the questions from I.

Paying the Bills

GOAL ▶ Arrange and cancel utilities

A **Discuss the questions with your classmates.**

1. What are utilities?

2. What utilities do you pay for?

3. If you rent, does your landlord pay for any utilities?

4. What information can you find on your utility bills?

Information Questions 🎧

What's your address?

Where do you live?

When will you be moving?

B **INTERPRET** **Read the gas bill and answer the questions.**

Southern Texas Gas

View Past Bills | Reading My Bill | Billing FAQs | Contact Us

Billing Date	Account Number	Billing Period	Total Amount Due
6/29	89100710875	5/23–6/27	$33.50

Name Vu Nguyen
Service Address 3324 Maple Road
Cedarville, TX 77014

Summary of Charges			
Customer Charge	33 days	x 0.16438=	5.42
Baseline	15 Therms	x 0.65133=	14.77
Over Baseline	10 Therms	x 0.82900=	13.29
Gas Charges			33.48
State Regulatory Fee 25 Therms		x 0.00076=	.02
Taxes and Fees on Gas Charges			.02
Total Gas Charges Including Taxes and Fees			$33.50
Thank you for your payment 6/06			$37.65
Current payment due by 7/25.			

Life
ONLINE

Most companies offer a "paperless bill" option. This means you will not receive a paper bill in the mail. You can go online and create an account to access your digital bill.

1. What is Vu's account number? _____

2. How much is their gas bill this month? _____

3. How much did they pay last month? _____

4. Which bill was more expensive: this month's or last month's? _____

5. When is the latest Vu can pay? _____

C Vu and his family are getting ready to move. Vu calls the electric company to speak to a customer service representative. Listen and write short answers for the following information. 🎧

1. Name of the company: _____

2. Name of the representative: _____

3. When Vu wants service turned off: _____

4. When Vu wants service turned on: _____

D **INTERPRET** Listen to the audio again and answer the questions. 🎧

1. The first voice is recorded and gives four choices. What are they?

    a. *get new service or cancel existing service* _____

    b. _____

    c. _____

    d. _____

2. What information does Vu give to the gas company?

    a. *his current address* _____

    b. _____

    c. _____

    d. _____

People are investing in alternative sources of power. This house has solar panels on the roof to help generate electricity.

E Study the chart.

Information Questions	
Question Words	**Example Questions**
How	**How** may I help you?
What	**What** is your current address?
When	**When** would you like your service turned off?

F Read and listen to the conversation. Underline the information questions.

Recording:	Thank you for calling Southern Texas Gas. Your call is very important to us. Please wait for the next available customer service representative.
Representative:	Hello, my name is Liam. How may I help you?
Vu:	Um, yes. My family is moving next week, and we need to have our gas turned off here and get the gas turned on in our new home.
Representative:	What is your current address?
Vu:	3324 Maple Road.
Representative:	What is your name, sir?
Vu:	Vu Nguyen.
Representative:	When would you like the gas turned off?
Vu:	Next Wednesday, please.
Representative:	And what is your new address?
Vu:	5829 Bay Road.
Representative:	And when would you like the gas turned on in your new home?
Vu:	This Monday, please.
Representative:	OK. Your current service will be turned off sometime on Wednesday the 11th, and your new service will be on before eight on Monday morning, the 9th. Is there anything else I can do for you?
Vu:	No, that's it.

G Practice the conversation in **F**. Make a new conversation using your own information. Remember to practice rising and falling intonation.

H EVALUATE With a partner, discuss ways to reduce the cost of your electric bill. What can you do to save energy?

How Much Can We Spend?

GOAL ▶ Create a budget

A What do you spend money on every month? Make a list.

_____rent_____   _____

_____   _____

_____   _____

_____   _____

B Share your list with a partner. Add anything that you forgot to your list.

C **INTERPRET** Listen to Mariana and Vu talk about their finances. Fill in the missing information. 🎧

INCOME	
Vu's Salary	$4,500
Mariana's Salary	_____
Total Income	_____

EXPENSES	
Rent	_____
Utilities	
Electricity	$100
Gas	_____
Cell phones	$85
Cable TV + Internet	$124.99
Streaming service	$19.99
Groceries	_____
Auto	
Gas and maintenance	_____
Car loan	_____
Total Expenses	_____

Life
ONLINE

Cable and internet bundle prices change. Make sure to check the prices of several providers to make sure you are getting the best deal. Sometimes it can be worth changing companies every couple of years–providers will give a discount to get customers back!

_____

D Answer the following questions about the Nguyens' budget with a partner.

1. What is their total income?

_____

2. What are their total expenses?

_____

3. How much extra cash do they have left after all the bills are paid? (*Hint:* Subtract total expenses from total income.)

_____

4. In your opinion, what are some things they forgot to budget for?

_____

5. What do you think they should do with their extra money?

_____

E **ILLUSTRATE** Look at the bar graph for the Nguyen family's expenses. Complete the graph with their expenses from **C**. Do not include rent.

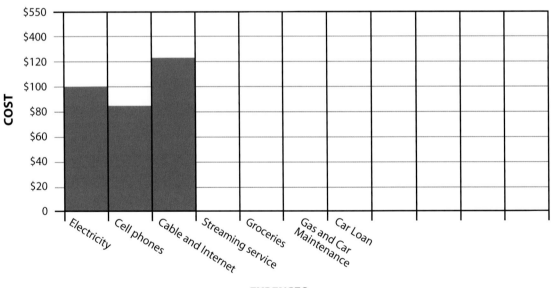

F Include any other items you think the Nguyens should add to their budget and the amount for each in the graph.

G **APPLY** Work as a team to create a family budget. Use the following information:

- Your family has two adults and three children. The children are two, five, and eight.

- You live in a four-bedroom house that you rent.

- Both adults have full-time jobs.

- You have two cars, one that you own (no payments) and the other that you make payments on.

Decide what your total household income is. Fill in the amounts that you would spend each month on expenses, and make a realistic budget based on your total income.

INCOME	
Salary 1	_____
Salary 2	_____
Total Income	_____
EXPENSES	
Rent	_____
Utilities	_____
Electricity	_____
Gas	_____
Cell phones	_____
Cable and internet	_____
Streaming service	_____
Food	_____
Groceries	_____
Eating out	_____
Entertainment	_____
Auto	_____
Gas and maintenance	_____
Car loan	_____
Insurance	_____
Registration	_____
OTHER	
_____	_____
_____	_____
_____	_____
_____	_____
Total Expenses	_____

H **ILLUSTRATE** Use the information you provided in **G** to make a bar graph.

Tenant's Rights

GOAL ▶ Write a formal letter

A **DETERMINE** Look at the pictures. Do you ever have these problems in your home? Are you a do-it-yourself person or do you call someone to make repairs?

a. The air conditioner isn't working.

b. There are roaches and mice in the kitchen.

c. The electricity went out.

d. The faucet is leaking.

B Who can you call to fix each problem? Match the person with the problem.

1. __c__ electrician   2. _____ handyman

3. _____ exterminator   4. _____ plumber

C Practice the conversation with a partner. Use the situations in A to make new conversations.

Tenant:	Hello. This is <u>John</u> in Apartment 3B.
Landlord:	Hi, <u>John</u>. What can I do for you?
Tenant:	<u>The air conditioning in our apartment isn't working</u>. (*State the problem.*)
Landlord:	OK. I'll send <u>a handyman over to fix it tomorrow</u>. (*State the solution.*)
Tenant:	Thanks.

D **Indira had a bad night in her apartment. Read about what happened.** 🎧

I had a terrible night. While I was making dinner, I saw a mouse. Then the electricity went out while I was studying. It was dark, so I went to bed. But I couldn't sleep. The faucet was dripping all night. The neighbors were shouting and their dog was barking too. Perhaps I should move!

E **Study the charts. Then underline examples of the *past continuous* in the paragraph in D.**

Past Continuous			
Subject	*Be*	**Verb + *ing***	**Example Sentence**
I / He / She / It	was	making	I **was making** breakfast.
You / We / They	were	studying	They **were studying**.
Use the past continuous to talk about things that started in the past and continued for a period of time.			

Past Continuous Using *While*			
Subject	*Be*	**Verb + *ing***	**Example Sentence**
I / He / She / It	was	making	While I **was making** dinner, I saw a mouse.
You / We / They	were	studying	The electricity went out while we **were studying**.
To connect two events that happened in the past, use the past continuous with *while* for the longer event. Use the simple past for the shorter event. ***Note:*** You can reverse the two clauses, but you need a comma if the *while* clause comes first.			

F **Use *while* to combine the two sentences.**

1. He was sleeping. The phone rang.

   While he was sleeping, the phone rang. (or) The phone rang while he was sleeping.

2. Joshua was painting the cabinet. The shelf fell down.

   _____

3. I saw the crack in the wall. I was hanging a painting.

   _____

4. He was taking a shower. The water got cold.

   _____

G Vu Nguyen had a problem when his family first moved into their new apartment. Read the email that he sent to his landlord.

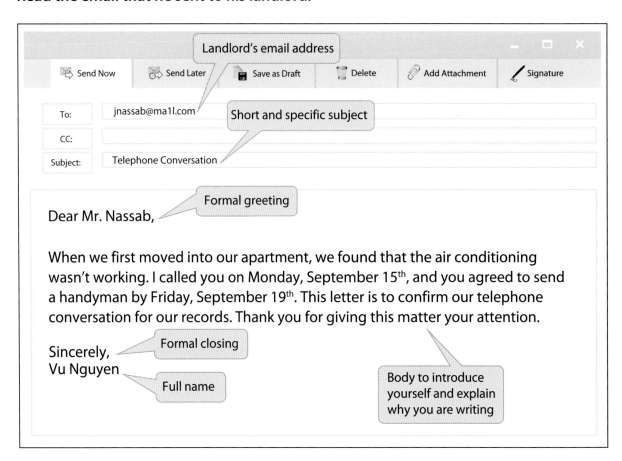

H What are the different parts of the email? Discuss them with your teacher.

I DETERMINE Work with a partner to brainstorm problems you can have in an apartment and share them with the class.

_____

_____

_____

_____

J APPLY Write an email to your landlord about a problem that you had in the past or a current problem you are having. Use Vu's email as an example.

K ANALYZE Exchange the email with a partner. Check your partner's email for grammar, spelling, and punctuation mistakes.

LESSON 6

Explore the Workforce

GOAL ▶ Compare property management careers

A Listen to the audio and fill in the missing words.

Property Management Industry Statistics

The property management job market should remain stable throughout the 2020s.

*   There are around 220,000 property _____ who work for property management _____.

*   The _____ wage is $73,210 per _____ or $35.20 per _____.

*   _____ pay is $59,660 per year or $28.68 per hour.

*   The _____ paid property managers earn $134,570 per year and the _____ paid earn $31,330 per year.

*   The average property manager at _____ has a _____ diploma or equivalent.

B Match and discuss the meanings with your teacher.

_____ 1. average   a. payment made to employee

_____ 2. median pay   b. equal

_____ 3. entry-level   c. in the middle

_____ 4. equivalent   d. payment in the middle range

_____ 5. wage   e. the lowest level of employment

_____ 6. stable   f. the same

C What are the different job opportunities in property management? Read.

Community Managers keep the community running smoothly. They help residents, oversee operations and services, and manage finances.

Leasing Consultants recruit new residents and match them with the right housing for their needs and budget. They help current residents by solving problems to make life better in the community.

Maintenance technicians maintain the property and keep everything in working order (plumbing, heating, cooling, locks, carpentry and more).

D **EVALUATE** Study the bar graph below. Look up any unknown words in your dictionary. Complete the chart with the jobs related to each service.

Common Property Management Services

Community Manager	Leasing Consultant	Maintenance Technician

E **COMPARE** Compare the salaries of the three positions. Work with a partner to write comparative sentences in your notebook.

EXAMPLE: A community manager makes less bonus pay than than a leasing consultant.

Leasing Consultant	Community Manager	Maintenance Technician
Annual Base Salary Range Entry Level: $30,900–$41,400 Experienced: $41,200–$60,200	***Annual Base Salary Range*** <150 units: $43,700–$60,900 150–300 units: $54,600–$73,900	***Annual Base Salary Range*** Entry Level: $35,300–$51,800 Maintenance Supervisor: $50,100–$67,000
Additional Earnings Bonus Pay: 17.8–20.3% of salary	***Additional Earnings*** Bonus Pay: 15.6–19.7% of salary	***Additional Earnings*** Overtime and Bonus Pay: 6.9–11.7% of salary
	Housing Benefits Some employers offer rent reductions of 20% or more.	***Housing Benefits*** Some employers offer rent reductions of 20% or more.

F Read the online job ad and work with a partner to answer the questions that follow.

WANTED

On-Site Residential Property Manager for 20 units in Gardena, CA

Must live onsite and have a minimum of one year of management/maintenance experience with references.

Compensation will be a fully-remodeled one-bedroom apartment + $2,500.00 per month salary. Must be bilingual in Spanish.

Responsibilities:

- Collect rent
- Handle tenant complaints
- Maintain common areas
- Clean vacant units
- Move-in and move-out inspections
- Enforce apartment rules
- Oversee outside vendors

What email should the hiring manager reach you at?

Enter your email   *Apply Now*

1. What is the title of the job?
2. What experience is necessary?
3. What is the pay?
4. What are three of the responsibilities?
5. Are references required?
6. Would you apply for this job? Why or why not?

Review

A **Rewrite the classified ad to describe a place where you would want to live.**

Three-bedroom apartment with a large kitchen, two-car garage, washer / dryer, and new appliances. Apartment is located near the beach.

$2,500 per month
$500 security deposit

Contact Agent

_____

_____

_____

_____

_____

_____

B **Complete the sentences with *more* or *most* (+) or *fewer, less, fewest,* or *least* (–).**

1. (+) Kim's house has _____*more*_____ entrances than Jen's house.

2. (+) The blue condo has _____ bathrooms than the yellow one.

3. (+) Octavio's apartment gets the _____ light.

4. (–) That condo has _____ balconies than this one.

5. (–) Their house has the _____ furniture.

6. (+) Andrew's place has _____ rooms than Brad's place.

7. (–) The small apartment has _____ patio space than the big one.

8. (+) The Jacksons' apartment has the _____ appliances.

Learner Log	I can interpret classified ads.
	☐ Yes ☐ No ☐ Maybe

C Write *Yes / No* questions to ask your partner about his or her dream home. Then ask your partner the questions and write the answers.

1. Q: _____

   A: _____

2. Q: _____

   A: _____

3. Q: _____

   A: _____

4. Q: _____

   A: _____

D Look at the ad you wrote in **A** and the answers you got from your partner in **C**. Write sentences comparing the two dream homes.

EXAMPLE: *My partner's dream home has fewer bedrooms than my dream home.*

1. _____

   _____

2. _____

   _____

3. _____

   _____

4. _____

   _____

E Imagine you are moving to a new city. What utilities will you have to call and order? With a partner, role-play a phone conversation with a customer service representative.

Learner Log	I can make decisions.	I can arrange and cancel utilities.
	Yes No Maybe	Yes No Maybe

F Think about your monthly expenses and complete the budget below.

INCOME	
Salary	_____
Total Income	_____

EXPENSES	
Rent	_____
Utilities	
Gas	_____
Cell phones	_____
Cable and internet	_____
Streaming service	_____
Other	_____
Groceries	_____
Eating out	_____
Entertainment	_____
Auto	_____
Gas and maintenance	_____
Car loan	_____
Insurance	_____
Registration	_____
Total Expenses	_____

G Use the simple past and the past continuous to complete the sentences.

1. The light _____ (go out) while Mariana
   _____ (take) a shower.

2. A spider _____ (drop) onto my arm while
   I _____ (eat) dinner.

3. While Marie _____ (study), the landlord
   _____ (call).

H Think of some problems you have with the place where you live. On a piece of paper, use one of your ideas to write a letter to your landlord.

I Highlight ten new words you want to study in the unit. Write the words and definitions on index cards. In pairs, choose a card and ask questions to guess the word on the card.

Learner Log	I can create a budget.	I can write a formal letter.
	☐ Yes ☐ No ☐ Maybe	☐ Yes ☐ No ☐ Maybe

Create a Housing Plan

SOFT SKILL ▶ Active Listening

With a team, you will create a housing plan, a budget, and a classified ad for where you will live.

1. **COLLABORATE** Form a team of four or five students. Choose positions for each member of your team.

Position	Job Description	Student Name(s)
Student 1: Leader	Check that everyone speaks English. Check that everyone participates.	
Student 2: Secretary	Write the classified ad with help from your team.	
Student 3: Financial Planner	Create the budget.	
Students 4/5: Family Representatives	Plan a presentation of your housing plan.	

2. Think about your family's needs. Create your family budget.

3. Identify a neighborhood you would like to live in. Write a classified ad for a home in that community.

4. Make a list of all the utilities you will need to arrange for.

5. Create a poster with artwork. Include your budget, classified ad, and list of utilities.

6. Present your poster to the class.

Active Listening:

Listen attentively

Listen carefully while each team is presenting. Put your phone down. Make sure to look at the speaker. Avoid having side conversations with a partner.

A building with a colorful mural in Soho, New York

Reading Challenge

C Read about tiny house living.

D Make a list of the advantages and disadvantages of tiny house living.

Advantages	Disadvantages
• *same amenities as regular-sized house*	

E **INFER** Make inferences.

1. Why are bills cheaper for tiny house owners?

2. Why do tiny house owners often go out to eat?

F Go online and look for tiny houses for sale in your area. How much do they cost?

Tiny House Living

A recent trend in the US is tiny houses. A tiny house is usually 300 to 500 square feet and many times, these tiny houses have wheels so they can be moved around to any location. Sounds great, doesn't it? While there are many advantages to living in a tiny house, there are also some disadvantages.

5   A tiny house is just like any other house, except smaller. It has all the amenities of a regular-sized house, such as air conditioning, a washer / dryer, a stovetop, and sometimes a bathtub. Also, building a tiny house is much cheaper (average cost $30,000 to $75,000), and once it's done, you will have fewer and less expensive bills. And imagine how little cleaning you will have to do if your house is smaller! Tiny houses require that you downsize and live a simpler life.

10   A tiny house may sound like a good idea, but it may not be the best life for everyone. Having a smaller space means not a lot of storage, no buying in bulk, and no room for leftovers. Cooking will take some getting used to with your small counterspace and smaller oven. And with your smaller kitchen and cabinets, you will be going to the store often. Many tiny house owners end up eating out instead of cooking at home. If you like to entertain, you will have less space for guests.

15 And you may be cleaning all the time because your tiny house can look cluttered very quickly.

    Only you can decide if tiny house living is right for you and your family. You must think about the pros and cons and decide if it's a lifestyle for you. But wouldn't it be fun to have your house on wheels and wake up in the mountains one morning and on the beach the next?

This is the interior of a narrow boat which is also a tiny home.

4 Our Community

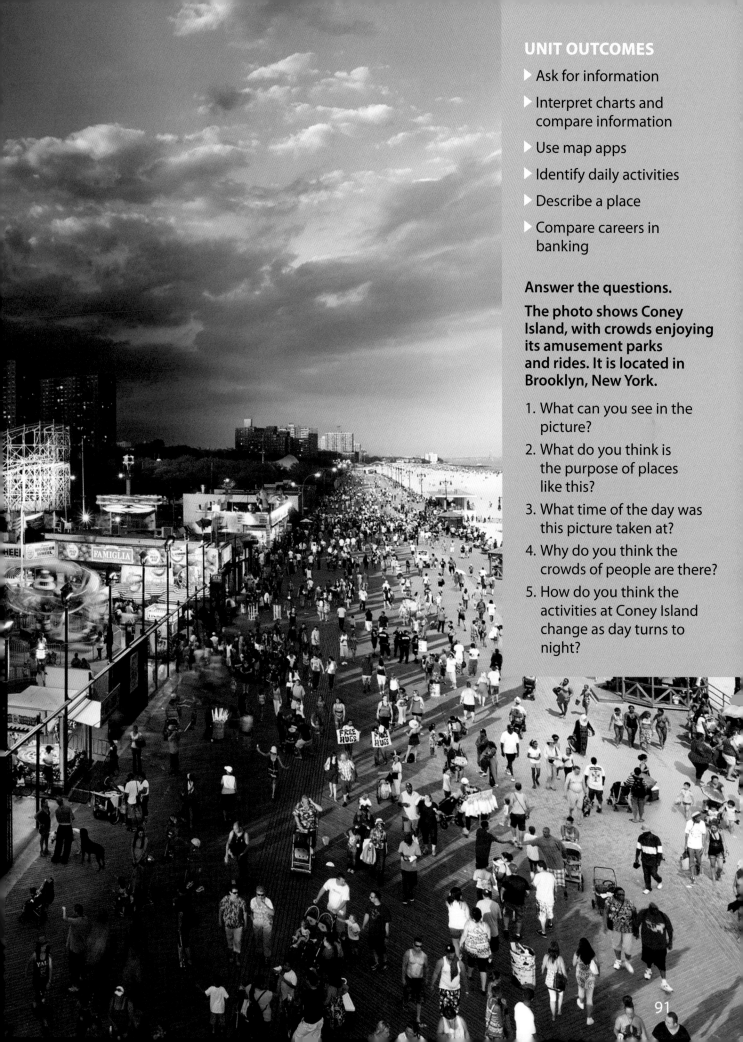

UNIT OUTCOMES

▶ Ask for information

▶ Interpret charts and compare information

▶ Use map apps

▶ Identify daily activities

▶ Describe a place

▶ Compare careers in banking

Answer the questions.

The photo shows Coney Island, with crowds enjoying its amusement parks and rides. It is located in Brooklyn, New York.

1. What can you see in the picture?

2. What do you think is the purpose of places like this?

3. What time of the day was this picture taken at?

4. Why do you think the crowds of people are there?

5. How do you think the activities at Coney Island change as day turns to night?

Places in Your Community

GOAL ▶ Ask for information

A Gloria and her family are new to the community. Read her list of things to do. Where does Gloria need to go for each one? Listen and write the names of the places. 🎧

The Post Office at the
James A. Farley Building
in New York City

1. Find a place for my children to play sports   _____

2. Register for an ESL class   _____

3. Open a checking account   _____

4. Register my car and get a new license   _____

5. Mail some packages back home   _____

6. Pick up some bus schedules   _____

B **DEMONSTRATE** Practice the conversation with a partner. Use the information in **A** to make new conversations.

Student A: Where can I <u>get a new driver's license?</u>

Student B: At the <u>DMV</u>.

DMV
DMV = Department of Motor Vehicles

C **Study the chart.**

Information Questions		
Location	Where How far What	is the bank? is the school from here? is the address?
Time	When What time How often	does the library open? does the restaurant close? do the buses run?
Cost	How much	does it cost?

D **Match the questions you ask local businesses with the answers.**
Which information could you find online?

____*g*____ 1. How often do the buses run?

_____ 2. Where's your restaurant?

_____ 3. How much does it cost?

_____ 4. What's his address?

_____ 5. What time do you close?

_____ 6. How far is the store from here?

_____ 7. When do you open?

_____ 8. What time do you close on Sunday?

a. We open at 10 a.m.

b. It's about five miles away.

c. We close at 10 p.m.

d. We're open from 10 a.m. to 6 p.m. on Sunday.

e. His address is 71 South Pine Avenue.

f. It's on the corner of 7th and Pine.

g. They run every 20 minutes.

h. It costs $50 to service your computer.

Life
ONLINE
It is usually faster to research information on your cell phone or computer.

E **Practice asking and answering the questions in D with a partner.**

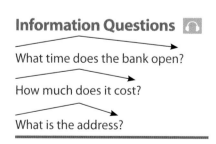

Information Questions

What time does the bank open?

How much does it cost?

What is the address?

F DETERMINE Write questions Gloria needs to ask local businesses to match the answers below.

1. *What time does the bank open?* _____ The bank opens at 9:00 a.m.

2. _____ A driver's license costs $39.

3. _____ The library is about a mile from here.

4. _____ The trains run every ten minutes.

5. _____ You can return books anytime.

6. _____ The DMV is at 112 Main Street.

7. _____ The children's book section is upstairs.

G Complete the conversations with a logical question or answer. Practice the conversations with a partner.

Conversation 1

Student A: Good morning. This is Food Mart.

Student B: _____

Student A: We're open now.

Student B: Great! Thank you.

Conversation 2

Student A: Thank you for calling The Book Stop. How can I help you?

Student B: _____

Student A: 4635 Broadway.

Student B: And when do you close?

Student A: _____

Student B: Thanks!

H APPLY Write a to-do list like the one Gloria made in **A** in your notebook. Write the place where you can go in your community to get the task done. Also, write some questions to ask.

To-do	Place	Questions
get information about ESL classes	adult education center	When do classes start? Where is the school?

The Bank, the Library, and the DMV

GOAL ▶ Interpret charts and compare information

A **Discuss the following banking words with your classmates and teacher.**

ATM	debit card	minimum deposit	secure banking
average daily balance	minimum daily balance	online banking	unlimited

B **Riverview Bank offers three kinds of checking accounts. Interpret the website below.**

Riverview BANK™	Riverview Total Checking	Riverview Secure Banking	Riverview Premier Plus Checking
With a Riverview bank account, you'll enjoy state-of-the-art online banking and world-class customer service.			
Access to Riverview ATMs	yes	yes	yes
Online Banking, Online Bill Pay, and Mobile Banking	yes	yes	yes
Fees waived at non-Riverview ATMs	no	no	yes
Debit card	yes	yes	yes
Fees waived for checks	no	no paper checks	yes
Monthly service fee	$12 (fee waived if $500 in electronic deposits per month or $1,500 balance)	$4.95	$25 (fee waived if $15,000 total balance)

C **Practice asking questions about the bank information above with a partner.**

1. Can you do online bill pay with the _____ account?

2. What is the monthly service fee for the _____ account?

3. Do you get a debit card with the _____ account?

4. Can you use non–Riverview ATMs for free with the _____ account?

D **DECIDE** **Listen to each person talk about their banking habits. Decide which account above would be best for each one of them.** 🎧

Life
ONLINE Watch the video at the end of the unit to learn about useful bank tips, including two-factor authentication and recognizing scams.

E INFER Look at the Seal Beach Library website.

Seal Beach Digital Library
FREE WITH YOUR LIBRARY CARD

🔍 Search

| Ebooks | Audiobooks | News | Movies | Research | eLearning | Career Help |

Our library has great resources for students of all ages that are fun, interesting, and educational! They are free to use. All you need is your library card.

Click on one of the buttons above and select one of the resources that pop up. When you click on any of the resources in our Digital Library, you will be leaving the Seal Beach Public Library's website.

With our online resources you can read a book, newspaper, or magazine. You can take classes to learn something new or get help with homework. You can also take practice tests and get career help with things such as writing a resume. You can even research your family tree!

DAILY NEWS
EXTRA! EXTRA
WORLD NEWS

F You can use many of the library services without going into the library. If you wanted to find information on each of the following, what tab would you click in E?

1. Find out more about the US government. ___Research___

2. Listen to *To Kill a Mockingbird* by Harper Lee. _____

3. Read your local newspaper. _____

4. Practice job interview techniques. _____

5. Find a textbook and read it online. _____

6. Watch a movie with your grandchildren. _____

7. Get help writing a resume for a new job. _____

8. Learn a new language. _____

G Find your local library online. Does it offer the same digital resources?

H Have you been to the DMV in your city? If so, why did you go there? Did you have to pay for services? Look at the chart of DMV fees below.

	Type	Fee
New	Driver's license	$48
	Learner's permit (valid for 18 months)	$32
	State ID card	$28
	Senior citizen (65 or older) ID card	no fee
Renewal	Driver's license	$48
	State ID card	$28
Replacement	Driver's license	$25
	Learner's permit	$22
	State ID card	$18

I Read about each person below and write how much they will have to pay.

1. Enrico needs to get a new state ID card. $ _____

2. Liza lost her learner's permit, and she needs to get a new one. $ _____

3. Feng's driver's license expired, and he needs to get a new one. $ _____

4. Aina and Claudia just learned how to drive, and they both need to get new driver's licenses. $ _____

5. Gertrude is 65 and needs to get a state ID card. $ _____

J **CREATE** Choose one place in your community: a bank, a library, or the DMV. In a small group, create a one-page information sheet.

The Provincetown Public Library in Provincetown, Massachusetts is a historical building at the center of the community.

Finding Places

GOAL ▶ Use map apps

A **Look at the picture. What is it? Discuss and answer the questions.**

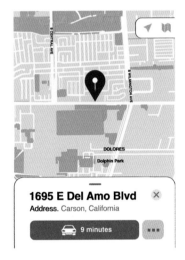

1695 E Del Amo Blvd
Address. Carson, California

🚗 9 minutes

1. What address is this person going to?

_____

2. Is this person walking or driving?

_____

3. How long will it take to get there?

_____

4. What city is this address in?

_____

B **Map apps show different modes of transportation. Match the symbols to their meaning.**

a.   b.   c.   d. ![walking] e.

_____ walking   _____ using a ride share app   _____ riding a bike

_____ taking the bus   _____ driving a car

C **The app shows you the different routes. Choose the best answer below.**

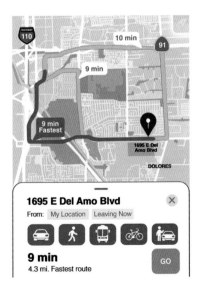

1695 E Del Amo Blvd
From: My Location Leaving Now

🚗 🚶 🚌 🚲 🚗

9 min
4.3 mi. Fastest route   GO

1. There are two highways / freeways on this map. The route choices suggest you take _____.

   a. 110   b. 91   c. neither

2. The fastest route will take you _____.

   a. 9 minutes   b. 15 minutes   c. 10 minutes

3. The app gives you _____ route choices.

   a. 1   b. 2   c. 3

D Once you are moving, the map gives you step-by-step directions to your destination. Ask and answer the questions with a partner.

EXAMPLE: **A:** How fast can I drive?
B: The speed limit is 40 miles per hour.

1. What street am I driving on?

2. How much longer do I continue straight?

3. What am I going to do next?

4. What time will we get there?

5. How many miles away is it?

E Study the map of San Diego below. What symbols do you see?

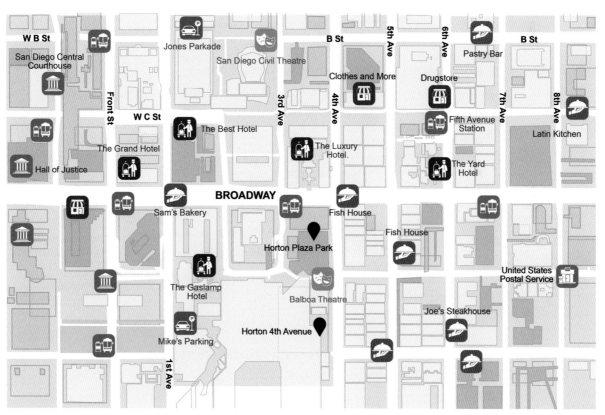

F Write the correct word on the line.

bus stop	hotel	post office	store
courthouse	parking lot	restaurant	theater

1. _____

2. _____

3. _____

4. _____

5. _____

6. _____

7. _____

8. _____

G Study these expressions for giving directions in a city.

Go straight for three blocks.	It's next to the bank.
Turn left. / Make a left.	It's across from the park.
Take Broadway to Sixth Avenue.	It's on the corner of Front Street and West C Street.

H Read the directions and follow them on the map in **E** with your finger.

Start at the courthouse. Walk down to Broadway and turn left. Walk 7 blocks until you get to 6th Ave. Turn right. Walk one block to E street. Turn left and walk two blocks. What is the building on the corner? _____

I Using the map in **E**, give a partner directions to different places. Start your conversations using the questions below.

	the Balboa Theater		the Pastry Bar?
How can I get to	the post office	from	the Hall of Justice?
	Sam's Bakery		the drugstore?
	the Grand Hotel		the Luxury Hotel?

Getting Things Done!

GOAL ▶ Identify daily activities

A Listen to Gloria talk about her busy morning. 🎧

Yesterday was a busy day! After I went for an early morning run, I got the kids ready for school. Before my husband left for work, we planned what to cook for dinner. When everyone left the house, I made my list of errands, and off I went. First, I returned some books to the library. I stopped by the bank to make a deposit after I returned the books. Then, I went to the post office to mail a package to my family back in Brazil. The next errand on my list was grocery shopping. But, before I went grocery shopping, I remembered to go to the cleaner's and pick up some skirts. And finally, when I finished shopping, I went home.

B **SEQUENCE** Listen again and number the activities in the correct order.

_____ picked up dry cleaning   _____ made a list of errands

_____ got the kids ready for school   _____ mailed a package at the post office

_____ planned dinner   _____ returned books to the library

_____ went to the bank to make a deposit _____ went back home

___1___ went for a run   _____ went grocery shopping

Shopping at the Farmer's Market
is a way to get fresh produce.

C *Before, after,* and *when* are used to connect two ideas and show their relationship in time.

Adverbial Clauses with *Before, After,* and *When*	
Rule	**Example Sentences**
A comma separates an adverbial clause that comes before the main clause.	**Before I went grocery shopping,** I stopped by the dry cleaner's to pick up some skirts. **After I returned the books,** I stopped by the bank to make a deposit. **When everyone left the house,** I made my list of errands.
A comma is not used when the adverbial clause comes after the main clause.	I stopped by the dry cleaner's to pick up some skirts **before I went grocery shopping.** I stopped by the bank to make a deposit **after I returned the books.** I made a list of errands **when everyone left the house.**

D Underline the action that happened first in each of the sentences.

1. After I woke up, I made breakfast.

2. I stopped by the bank to make a deposit before I returned the books.

3. Before Abebi went shopping, she went to the gym.

4. When my kids came home, I made dinner.

E Rewrite each sentence above, switching the order of the two actions.

1. **After** I woke up, I made breakfast.

   I made breakfast after I woke up. _____

2. _____

3. _____

4. _____

F ANALYZE Talk with your partner. In the sentences you wrote in E, which action happened first?

G Write sentences with adverbial clauses. Use the words in parentheses. Then reverse the clauses and rewrite the sentences.

1. Ali finished work. He went out with his friends. (when)

   a. _When Ali finished work, he went out with his friends._

   b. _Ali went out with his friends when he finished work._

2. Yasu saved enough money. He bought a new bicycle. (after)

   a. _____

   b. _____

3. The alarm went off. Maya jumped out of bed. (when)

   a. _____

   b. _____

4. I cleaned the house. I washed my car. (before)

   a. _____

   b. _____

H APPLY Think of things you did yesterday and the order in which you did them. Write three sentences using *before*, *after*, and *when* to talk about your day. Share with a partner.

1. _____

   _____

2. _____

   _____

3. _____

   _____

Pausing

Pausing is taking a breath in the middle of the sentence.
We usually pause between two thoughts or when there is a comma.

                              pause
                                 ∨
When my kids came home, I made dinner.

                              pause
                                 ∨
She went to the store before she picked up the dry cleaning.

My Town

GOAL ▶ Describe a place

A Gloria is writing a paragraph about Lindon, the town where she lives. Read her brainstorming notes below.

Reasons I love Lindon

safe neighborhoods (kids play in park)   affordable housing (can buy a new house)

good schools (nationally recognized)   ~~good shopping~~

~~mild weather (never gets too cold or hot)~~   good job opportunities (computer industry)

Brainstorm

generate a list of ideas

B **SEQUENCE** Gloria is writing her paragraph. The six sentences below are not in the correct order. Choose the best topic sentence and write *1*. Choose the best conclusion sentence and write *6*. Then order the support sentences from *2–5*.

_____5_____ Thanks to the great job market in Lindon, my husband got an excellent position in a computer company.

_____ Our family can buy a nice house because the housing prices are very affordable here.

_____ I love Lindon so much that I can't imagine moving.

_____ The neighborhoods are very safe, so I can let my children play in the park with other children.

_____ The excellent schools in this area are nationally recognized.

_____ There are many reasons I love Lindon.

C Compose a paragraph using Gloria's sentences in **B**. Use transitions from the box below to connect the support sentences. Write a title for Gloria's paragraph on the top line.

First of all,	Second of all,	Third,	Also,
First,	Second,	Furthermore,	Finally,

_____

_____

_____

_____

_____

_____

_____

_____

_____

D **FORMULATE** Now think about your town. Follow each step below.

1. Brainstorm reasons why you like your town.

Reasons I love _____

friendly people

2. Choose four reasons *from your list* about why you like your town to include in your paragraph.

3. Write a topic sentence for your paragraph.

_____

_____

_____

4. Write four support sentences based on the four reasons you chose.

a. _____

_____

_____

b. _____

_____

_____

c. _____

_____

_____

d. _____

_____

_____

5. Write a conclusion sentence.

_____

_____

_____

E **COMPOSE** On a piece of paper, write a paragraph about your town or city using the information in **D**. Use transitions to connect your ideas. Give your paragraph a title.

Explore the Workforce

GOAL ▶ Compare careers in banking

A Imagine you want to work in a bank. Answer the following questions in a small group.

1. What are the job choices in a bank?

2. What skills are needed to be a bank employee?

3. What character traits are needed to be a bank employee?

B Look at the graph below. What does it show? Come up with a title for this graph and write it below.

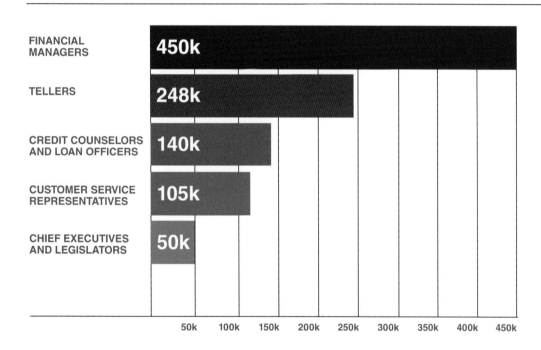

C **ANALYZE** Choose the correct answer.

1. How many people work as customer service representatives?

   a. 50,000   b. 105,000   c. 140,000   d. 245,000

2. Which job has the most people in the workforce?

   a. financial managers   b. credit counselors

   c. chief executives   d. customer service representatives

3. Which job has the least people in the workforce?

    a. tellers   c. credit counselors

    b. chief executives   d. customer service representatives

4. Which two jobs have over 200,000 people in the workforce?

    a. tellers + chief executives   c. credit counselors + financial managers

    b. tellers + financial managers   d. customer service representatives + financial managers

D   **INTERPRET**   **What does a bank teller do? Read and interpret the data below with your teacher.**

Bank Teller	
2020 Median Pay	$32,620 per year $15.68 per hour
Typical Entry-Level Education	High school diploma or equivalent
Work Experience in a Related Occupation	None
On-the-job Training	Short-term on-the-job training
Number of Jobs, 2020	248,500
Job Outlook, 2020–30	–17% (Decline)
Employment Change, 2020–30	–73,100

A bank teller, or bank clerk, is an employee who helps clients with routine financial transactions, such as making deposits, handling withdrawals, and issuing money orders or cashier's checks to bank customers.

E   **Decide if each statement is *True* or *False*. If false, make it true.**

fewer

EXAMPLE: There will be ~~more~~ bank teller jobs in 2030. _____False_____

1. You can make almost $16 an hour as a bank teller. _____

2. The number of bank teller jobs is increasing. _____

3. You need a college degree to be a bank teller. _____

4. The bank will train you for this job. _____

5. You need previous experience to be a bank teller. _____

6. You can make $40,000 a year as a bank teller. _____

F   **Based on the information in D, do you think it will be easy to find a job as a bank teller? Why or why not?**

G COMPARE Look at the job ads for bank tellers. What are the similarities? Differences?

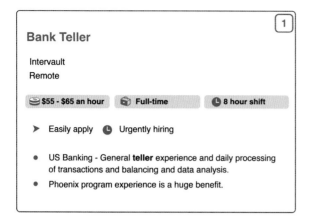

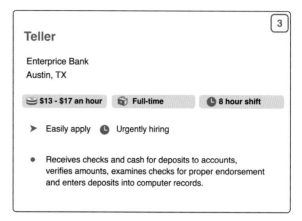

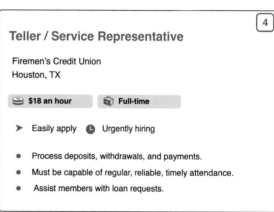

H Circle the correct ad numbers. More than one can be correct.

1. Which companies are hiring part time?

   a. Ad 1   b. Ad 2   c. Ad 3   d. Ad 4

2. Which job pays the best?

   a. Ad 1   b. Ad 2   c. Ad 3   d. Ad 4

3. Which companies are hiring urgently?

   a. Ad 1   b. Ad 2   c. Ad 3   d. Ad 4

4. Which companies are hiring full-time?

   a. Ad 1   b. Ad 2   c. Ad 3   d. Ad 4

5. Which ad mentions education?

   a. Ad 1   b. Ad 2   c. Ad 3   d. Ad 4

6. Which company is concerned about the employee being on time?

   a. Ad 1   b. Ad 2   c. Ad 3   d. Ad 4

I Which job would you apply for? Why? Tell your partner.

Review

A **Where can you do the following things in your community?**

1. have lunch _____

2. get medicine _____

3. mail a letter _____

4. get cash _____

B **Write questions you might ask at the places you wrote in A.**

1. _____

2. _____

3. _____

4. _____

C **Look back at the bank brochure on page 95. Read and decide which checking account would be the best for each person.**

1. Vim really wants an account with no service fee. He uses the ATM and doesn't want to pay for ATM transactions. He's saving up to buy a truck, and he has some money in a money market account. All of his accounts total over $30,000.

   Which account is best for Vim?

   _____

2. Mario likes to do his banking online and use the app on his phone. He uses direct deposit and never goes to the ATM. He uses his debit card for most transactions.

   Which account is best for Mario?

   _____

3. Gloria and her husband want to buy a new house. They currently have $15,600 in the bank. Gloria likes to go into the bank and speak with a teller, but her husband mostly uses the ATM for deposits and withdrawals.

   Which account is best for Gloria and her husband?

   _____

Learner Log	I can ask for information.	I can interpret charts and compare information.
	☐ Yes ☐ No ☐ Maybe	☐ Yes ☐ No ☐ Maybe

D Draw a map showing the way from your school to a nearby restaurant. Then write the directions. Read the directions to your partner and see if they can draw the map.

E Write sentences with adverbial clauses. Use *before, after,* or *when*.

1. I woke up. I made breakfast.

   After I woke up, I made breakfast.

2. I got some money out of the ATM. I bought some groceries.

3. Mala finished work. She went to the movies.

4. Luigi graduated from college. He got a job with a computer company.

Learner Log	I can use map apps.	I can identify daily activities.
	Yes No Maybe	Yes No Maybe

Review

F Ask your partner why they like the city they live in. Write four reasons below.

> Reasons my partner loves _____

G Write a short paragraph about your partner's city. Use transitions.

H Share the paragraph with your partner. Have your partner point to the topic sentence, support sentences, and conclusion sentence.

I Write ten new words you learned in this unit in your notebook. Put them in alphabetical order. Then look up the new words in a dictionary to see if the order was correct. Write sentences to help you remember the most difficult words.

Learner Log I can describe a place.
☐ Yes ☐ No ☐ Maybe

Create a Community Brochure

SOFT SKILL ▶ Active listening

Imagine that a new family has moved into your neighborhood and you want to tell them all about your community. With your team, create a brochure about your community.

1. Form a team of four or five students. Choose a position for each member of your team.

Position	Job Description	Student Name(s)
Student 1: Leader	Check that everyone speaks English. Check that everyone participates.	
Student 2: Writer	Write information for brochure with help from the team.	
Student 3: Designer	Design brochure layout and add artwork.	
Students 4/5: City Representatives	Help writer and designer with their work.	

2. Make a list of everything you want to include in your brochure, for example: information about the library, banks, and other local services.

3. Create the text for your community brochure.

4. Create a map of your community. Then create artwork for your community brochure.

5. Present your brochure to the class.

Active Listening
Listen carefully

Listen carefully while each team is presenting. How is their presentation different than yours? How is it the same?

Public sculptures, like The Bean in Chicago, are great places for people to meet in towns and cities.

Reading Challenge

A Look at the photo. Where is Hakki? Why is he on the floor? What are the other people in the photo doing?

B What do you think this quote means? Write an explanation and then share with a partner.

"Don't give to get, give to inspire others to give."

_____

_____

_____

_____

C Read the text.

D There are five examples of philanthropy in the reading. Underline and number them. Talk to your partner about a time when you were philanthropic.

E A synonym is a word that has a similar meaning to another word. There are three synonyms for the word "hard" in the reading. Find them and write them below.

Philanthropist

A philanthropist is someone who helps others, usually by donating money or physical items to those in need. Do you know a philanthropist? Do you think you are philanthropic?

1. Line 2 _____

2. Line 3 _____

3. Line 8 _____

F Hakki had some challenging experiences in his life. Write a short paragraph about a hard experience in your life, using the synonyms above.

_____

_____

_____

_____

_____

_____

Giving Back 🎧

Born in a small village in Turkey, Hakki Akdeniz never imagined he would be able to help others one day. His life was difficult. He had to polish shoes and sell things on the street to help support his family. Even though his life was challenging, he always dreamed of something more.

5   Luckily, he was able to move to Montreal, Canada, where his brother lived. There, he worked in his brother's pizzeria and learned the business. But he had bigger dreams than working for someone else. So, at 21, even though he didn't speak English, he moved to New York with $240 in his pocket. Again, life was tough, and he spent many homeless nights sleeping in Grand Central Station. After struggling for many years, he opened his first pizza shop in 2009. He
10 worked hard and opened a second shop in 2010. By 2016, he had a total of seven pizzerias.

But Hakki never forgot what it was like to be poor. If he saw a homeless person on the street, he gave them free pizza. He eventually started a weekly handout on West 34th Street, giving out food and clothing. In 2012, hurricane Sandy hit New York City and he served the neighborhoods pizza. When Hurricane Maria hit Puerto Rico in 2017, he organized a relief effort
15 and shipped tons of food, water, and supplies to the island. His Wednesday handout has grown, serving 300-400 homeless people every Wednesday night. From Turkey to Canada and finally New York, Hakki has learned that when you help others, you also help yourself.

Three-time World Pizza Spinning Champion Hakki Akdeniz shows off his spinning talent.

Money In The Bank

Before You Watch

A Look at the photo. What is the woman in the photo doing? What type of things do you think she is doing on her phone? Is it safe for her to be using her phone in the subway?

B Check (✓) what is true for you. Then share your answers with a partner.

☐ 1. I shop online.

☐ 2. I order food online.

☐ 3. I check my bank account balance online.

☐ 4. I deposit checks online.

☐ 5. I pay my bills online.

☐ 6. I send money to my friends or family online.

C You are going to watch a video with advice about how to keep your money and information safe online. What tips do you think the video will give? Share with a partner.

While You Watch

D Watch the video. Check (✓) the things Alex talks about doing online.

☐ 1. making friends

☐ 2. shopping for shoes

☐ 3. ordering tacos

☐ 4. playing video games

☐ 5. buying shampoo

☐ 6. signing up for a new credit card

☐ 7. depositing checks

☐ 8. checking a bank account balance

☐ 9. paying bills

☐ 10. getting a debit card

☐ 11. sending money to friends and family

☐ 12. searching for ATMs

E Watch the video again. Complete the tips with the words you hear.

1. Never sign in to your _____ or enter your credit card number while using public wi-fi.

2. Don't give out your personal _____ over email or text.

3. Don't _____ on links in emails or texts if you don't know who sent them.

4. Use different _____ for different websites.

5. Check your _____ and bank account often to make sure there is nothing unusual.

After You Watch

F Read each sentence. Choose *T* if it is true and *F* if it is false.

1. In middle school, Alex wasn't allowed to use the internet.   **T**   **F**

2. Alex shops online and uses online banking because it's convenient.   **T**   **F**

3. Alex says the internet is very dangerous.   **T**   **F**

4. Seeing the lock icon next to a URL can help you decide if a website is safe.   **T**   **F**

5. Two-factor authentication can help keep your information safe even if someone has your password.   **T**   **F**

6. Alex says he won't shop online or use online banking in the future.   **T**   **F**

G Work with a partner. Write three tips you can remember from the video. Do you follow this advice in your own life? Is there anything you plan to do differently in the future?

_____

_____

_____

5 Health

UNIT OUTCOMES

▶ Identify parts of the body
▶ Communicate symptoms
▶ Identify and analyze health habits
▶ Analyze nutrition information
▶ Interpret fitness information
▶ Compare health-related careers

Answer the questions.

1. What activities are good for you?
2. What activities are not good for your health?

People participate in an outdoor yoga class while a woman sits on a bench reading at a park in Washington, DC.

1. How many people are participating in the yoga class?
2. What other activities can you see in the photo? Are they healthy activities?
3. Is the woman reading in the photo doing a healthy activity?

119

The Human Body

GOAL ▶ Identify parts of the body

A **Label the parts of the body using the words from the box.**

ankle	chin	finger	knee	shoulder	toe
chest	elbow	hip	neck	stomach	wrist

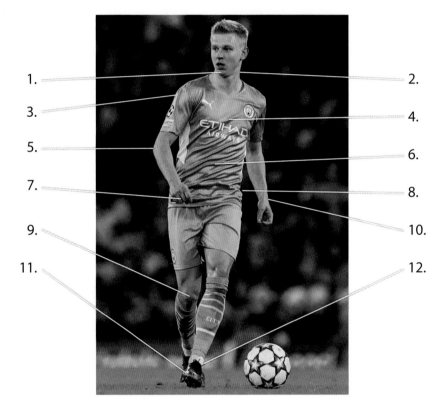

1. _____chin_____
2. _____
3. _____
4. _____
5. _____
6. _____
7. _____
8. _____
9. _____
10. _____
11. _____
12. _____

B **RECALL** **What other parts of the body can you name? Work with a partner. Label other parts of the body by drawing a line from the body part and writing its name.**

C Match the doctor with the specialization. Add one more to the list. Then compare answers with a partner.

___c___ 1. podiatrist   a. allergies and asthma

_____ 2. dermatologist   b. children

_____ 3. gynecologist/obstetrician   c. feet

_____ 4. cardiologist   d. teeth

_____ 5. ophthalmologist   e. mental health

_____ 6. pediatrician   f. heart

_____ 7. dentist   g. eyes

_____ 8. allergist   h. women and childbirth

_____ 9. psychiatrist   i. skin

_____10. _____   j. _____

D SUGGEST Talk with a partner. Use the statements to make recommendations about which type of doctor to see.

EXAMPLE: Student A: My mother's feet hurt.
            Student B: She should see a podiatrist.

1. My father is worried about his heart.   _____

2. My six-year-old daughter has a fever.   _____

3. My nose is running and my eyes are itchy.   _____

4. My eyes hurt when I read.   _____

5. I feel depressed.   _____

6. They have a rash on their necks.   _____

7. I think I have a cavity.   _____

8. _____   _____

E Look at the illustration of the internal parts of the human body. Practice saying the words with a partner.

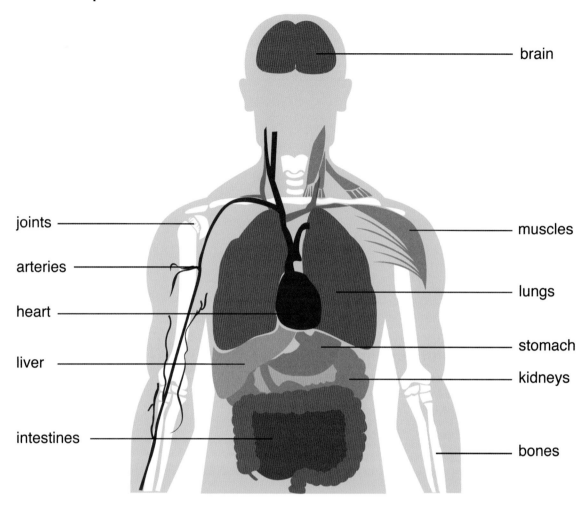

F Can you talk to your doctor about your medical history? Match the condition or disease with the correct part of the body. Then add one idea of your own.

1. __b__ high blood pressure

2. _____ asthma

3. _____ ulcers

4. _____ stroke

5. _____ arthritis

6. _____ _____

a. brain

b. heart and arteries

c. joints

d. stomach

e. lungs

f. _____

Illnesses and Symptoms

GOAL ▶ Communicate symptoms

A Read the conversation and answer the questions. 🎧

Doctor:	What seems to be the problem?
Ali:	I have a terrible backache.
Doctor:	I see. How long have you had this backache?
Ali:	I've had it for about a week.
Doctor:	Since last Monday?
Ali:	Yes, that's right.

1. What is the matter with Ali? _____

2. When did his problem start? _____

B Practice the conversations. Make new conversations using the pictures below.

Student A:	What's the matter?
Student B:	<u>I have a headache</u>.
Student A:	How long <u>have you had this headache</u>?
Student B:	<u>For five hours</u>.
Student A:	What's the matter?
Student B:	<u>My back hurts</u>.
Student A:	How long <u>has your back hurt</u>?
Student B:	<u>Since yesterday</u>.

Past Participle

Base Verb	Past Participle
be	been
have	had
feel	felt
hurt	hurt

1. I have a headache.
   (five hours)

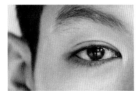

2. My eyes are red.
   (last night)

3. My shoulder hurts.
   (two weeks)

4. I feel tired.
   (Monday)

5. My throat is sore.
   (three days)

6. My back hurts.
   (yesterday)

C Study the chart with your teacher.

Present Perfect				
Subject	*Have*	**Past Participle**	**Illness**	**Example Sentence**
I / You / We / They	have	been felt	sick. ill.	I **have been** sick.
		had	a backache. a headache.	You **have had** a headache.
He / She / It	has	hurt	her arm. his leg.	He **has hurt** his leg.
Use the present perfect for events starting in the past and continuing up to the present.				

D Complete the sentences with the present perfect form of the verb in parentheses.

1. She _____ (be) tired since last week.

2. John's leg _____ (hurt) for three days.

3. Karen _____ (have) a sore throat since last night.

4. I _____ (feel) sick since Monday.

5. The girl's arm _____ (hurt) for two days.

6. The twins _____ (be) sick for a week.

E Study the chart with your teacher. Complete the sentences with *for* or *since*.

For—Length of Time	*Since*—Point in Time
five minutes three days one week two years a long time	last night Thursday November 2020 I was a child

1. I have been sick _____ Tuesday.

2. The boy's arm has hurt _____ a week.

3. You have felt ill _____ last night.

4. He has had a backache _____ two weeks.

F Make sentences using the present perfect and *for* or *since*. Listen and check your answers.

1. Ali has a backache / Monday

   Ali has had a backache since Monday.

2. I have a cold / three days

   _____

3. my leg hurts / last night

   _____

4. Julie feels dizzy / a week

   _____

5. Peter is sick / two weeks

   _____

G DESCRIBE Work in pairs. Write symptoms for each illness below.

Illness	Symptoms
a cold	
the flu	
a cough	
allergies	
depression	

H Practice the conversation. Make new conversations. Use the information from the chart in G.

Student A:	What's the matter?
Student B:	I'm coughing and sneezing.
Student A:	How long have you been coughing and sneezing?
Student B:	I've been coughing and sneezing for a week.
Student A:	Do you have a runny nose?
Student B:	Yes.
Student A:	Sounds like you might have a cold.

Health Habits

GOAL ▶ Identify and analyze health habits

A ANALYZE Look at the picture. What are the people doing? What is healthy and what is unhealthy?

B Match the health habits with the effects.

__j__ 1. be very stressed

_____ 2. drink too much alcohol

_____ 3. stay in the sun too long

_____ 4. eat junk food every day

_____ 5. exercise at least three times a week

_____ 6. not get enough calcium

_____ 7. not sleep eight hours every night

_____ 8. smoke too much

_____ 9. stay away from smoking

_____ 10. wear sunscreen

a. have healthy lungs

b. not be well rested

c. damage your liver

d. not have strong bones

e. get lung cancer

f. protect your skin

g. get skin cancer

h. be fit and healthy

i. gain weight

j. have high blood pressure

C Study the chart with your teacher.

Future Conditional Statements	
Cause: *If* + Present Form	**Effect: Future Form**
If you **are** very stressed,	you **will have** high blood pressure.
If you **don't get** enough calcium,	you **won't have** strong bones.
We can connect a cause and an effect by using a *future conditional* statement. The *if* clause (or the *cause*) is in the present tense and the *effect* is in the future tense.	
You **will have** high blood pressure	**if** you **are** very stressed.
You can reverse the clauses, but use a comma only when the *if* clause comes first.	

D Complete the sentences with the correct form of the verbs in parentheses.

1. If you _____wash_____ (wash) your hands a few times a day, you ___will not / won't get___ (not get) so many colds.

2. If Ann _____ (get) her teeth cleaned regularly, she _____ (not have) so many cavities.

3. My dad _____ (not lose) weight if he _____ (keep) eating foods that are high in fat.

4. My skin _____ (burn) if I _____ (not use) sunscreen.

5. If people _____ (not stretch) after they exercise, they _____ (have) sore muscles.

6. Bang Vu _____ (not be able to) talk tomorrow if he _____ (not rest) his voice.

Fast food is cheap and convenient, but it is unhealthy and can make people gain weight.

E With a partner, practice making conditional statements with the information from **B**. Use different subjects (*I, you, we, they, he, she, it*).

1. If we are very stressed, we will have high blood pressure.

2. _____

3. _____

4. _____

5. _____

6. _____

7. _____

F **REFLECT** Think about your good and bad health habits. Make two lists.

My Good Health Habits	My Bad Health Habits

G Write future conditional statements about good health habits that you want to have. Share your ideas with a partner and agree on the four most important ones.

1. If I get more sleep, I will concentrate better on my work.

2. _____

3. _____

4. _____

5. _____

6. _____

Nutrition Labels

GOAL ▶ Analyze nutrition information

A **MyPlate can help you make good decisions about daily food choices. Study the picture and answer the questions.**

1. Which food group should you eat the most of?

   _____

2. Which food group should you eat the least of?

   _____

B **Read the information in the table and answer the questions.**

Fruits	Eat a variety of fresh, canned, frozen, or dried fruit. Limit fruit juice.
Vegetables	Eat a variety of green vegetables like spinach and broccoli. Drink 100% vegetable juice.
Grains	Eat more whole grains. Grains are made from wheat, rice, oats, cornmeal, and barley.
Proteins	Eat a variety of lean proteins. Proteins are meat, poultry, seafood, beans, peas, eggs, nuts, and seeds.
Dairy	Consume dairy to help add calcium to your diet. Dairy products are made from milk.

1. Which food group is rice in? _____

2. Which food group are nuts in? _____

3. What is an example of a green vegetable? _____

4. Why do you think you should limit fruit juice? _____

C **EVALUATE** Read the tips for healthy eating. Check (✓) the tips you follow or would like to follow. Then discuss your answers with a partner.

Tips for Healthy Eating	Follow	Would Like to Follow
1. Keep raw vegetables in the refrigerator to eat as a snack.		
2. Eat a variety of foods to get all the nutrients you need.		
3. Eat lean meats like fish and chicken.		
4. Choose fat-free or low-fat dairy products.		
5. Try not to drink beverages with a lot of sugar such as soft drinks.		
6. Flavor foods with herbs and spices instead of salt.		
7. Pay attention to serving sizes.		
8. Choose foods that have less saturated fat.		

D **ANALYZE** Look at the nutrition label for macaroni and cheese.

Macaroni & Cheese Nutrition Facts

Amount Per Serving
Calories 250   Calories from Fat 110

	% Daily Value*
Total Fat 12g	18%
Saturated Fat 3g	15%
Cholesterol 30g	10%
Sodium 470mg	20%
Total Carbohydrate 31g	10%
Dietary Fiber 0g	0%
Sugars 5g	
Protein 5g	
Vitamin A	4%
Vitamin C	2%
Calcium	20%
Iron	4%

*Percent Daily Values are based on a 2,000 calorie diet. Your Daily Values may be higher or lower depending on your calorie needs.

E Listen to Darla explain nutritional information to her grandmother. 🎧

F Listen to each part of the conversation again and answer the questions. Check (✓) the box next to the correct answer. 🎧

1. What does Grandma need to look at if she wants to watch her salt intake?

   ☐ sodium   ☐ saturated fat

2. How many servings are in this box of macaroni and cheese?

   ☐ two   ☐ four

3. How many calories should an average adult have each day?

   ☐ 200   ☐ 2,000

4. What should Grandma avoid to have a healthy heart?

   ☐ cholesterol and saturated fat   ☐ carbohydrates and saturated fat

5. What should a diabetic look for on a food label?

   ☐ sugar   ☐ salt

6. What nutrient helps digestion?

   ☐ iron   ☐ fiber

G Read the nutrition guidelines and answer the questions about the macaroni and cheese label in D.

Recommended Amount of Calories and Fat Per Day
- 2,000 calories per day
- 20 or fewer grams saturated fat
- 65 grams total fat

Quick Guide to % Daily Value* for Nutrients
5% or less is LOW   20% or more is HIGH

*Percent Daily Values are based on a 2,000-calorie diet. Your Daily Values may be higher or lower depending on your calorie needs.

1. Is macaroni and cheese high in fat?

2. Is macaroni and cheese low in sodium?

3. Does it contain any protein? How much?

4. What vitamins does it contain? Is it high in vitamins?

5. Is macaroni and cheese a good source of calcium?

6. Do you think macaroni and cheese is a healthy food choice? Why or why not?

H **PLAN** Work with a partner and plan three meals based on MyPlate in A.

Healthy Living

GOAL ▶ Interpret fitness information

A **You are going to read a text about physical fitness. On a separate piece of paper, write one piece of advice that you think it will contain. Then read the article.** 🎧

Be physically active each day

Being physically active and maintaining a healthy weight are necessary for good health. Children, teens, adults, and the elderly can improve their health by including moderate physical activity in their daily lives.

Try to get at least 30 minutes (adults) or 60 minutes (children) of moderate physical activity most days of the week, preferably daily. No matter what activity you choose, you can do it all at once, or spread it out over the day.

How to make physical activity a regular part of your routine

Choose activities that you enjoy and that you can do regularly. Some people prefer activities that fit into their daily routines, like walking to the grocery store or gardening. Others prefer a regular exercise program, such as going to the gym or taking a weekly class. Some do both. The important thing is to be physically active every day.

B **Decide if the statements are *True* or *False*. Check (✓) the correct answers.**

	True	False
1. Physical exercise is necessary for good health.	☐	☐
2. Elderly people do not need to exercise.	☐	☐
3. Adults should exercise every day.	☐	☐
4. It is better to exercise throughout the day.	☐	☐
5. Gardening is a good way to exercise regularly.	☐	☐
6. The most important thing is to exercise regularly.	☐	☐

Life
ONLINE

Walking is a healthy exercise. The step counter on your phone is a useful way to check the amount of walking that you do.

C **Discuss these questions with your partner.**

1. Do you exercise more or less than recommended in the article?

2. Does your workplace offer physical activity programs? What are they?

D Look at the examples of physical activities. Which is an example of a routine activity? Which is an example of a recreational activity?

Mike rides his bicycle to the office every day.

Ana plays tennis twice a week with her friend.

E Read the list of routine activities. Check (✓) the activities you have tried. Put an *X* next to the activities you would like to try. Add two more activities.

☐ Walk or ride a bike to work

☐ Walk upstairs instead of taking an elevator

☐ Get off the bus a few stops early and walk the remaining distance

☐ Garden

☐ Push a stroller

☐ Clean the house

☐ Play actively with children

☐ Take a brisk ten-minute walk or bike ride in the morning, at lunch, and after dinner

☐ _____

☐ _____

F Read the list of recreational activities. Check (✓) the activities you have tried. Put an *X* next to the activities you would like to try. Add two more activities.

☐ Walk, jog, or cycle

☐ Swim or do water aerobics

☐ Play tennis or racquetball

☐ Do pilates or yoga

☐ Kayak or paddle board

☐ Hike

☐ Play basketball

☐ Dance

☐ Take part in an exercise program at work, home, school, or a gym

☐ _____

☐ _____

G Read the article. Then discuss the questions below with a partner. 🎧

Health Benefits of Physical Activity

Being physically active for at least 30 minutes on most days of the week reduces the risk of developing or dying of heart disease. It has other health benefits as well. No one is too young or too old to enjoy the benefits of regular physical activity.

Two types of physical activity are especially beneficial:

1) Aerobic activities: These are activities that speed your heart rate and breathing. They help cardiovascular fitness. Running, swimming, and walking are aerobic activities.

2) Activities for strength and flexibility: Developing strength may help build and maintain your bones. Carrying groceries and lifting weights are strength-building activities. Gentle stretching, dancing, or yoga can increase flexibility.

1. Why are aerobic activities good for you?

2. What are some examples of aerobic activities?

3. Why are activities for strength good for your bones?

4. What are some examples of strength-building activities?

5. What types of activities can increase your flexibility?

6. What are some activities you do for strength and flexibility?

H Read about more benefits of physical activity. Then discuss the questions with a partner.

More Health Benefits of Physical Activity

➤ Increases physical fitness
➤ Helps build and maintain healthy bones, muscles, and joints
➤ Builds endurance and muscular strength
➤ Helps manage weight

➤ Lowers risk factors for cardiovascular disease, colon cancer, and Type 2 diabetes
➤ Helps control blood pressure
➤ Promotes psychological well-being and self-esteem
➤ Reduces feelings of depression and anxiety

---

1. What diseases can exercise help prevent?

2. How does exercise help your circulatory system?

3. How does exercise affect your mood and your mental health?

4. What are some other benefits of exercise?

Explore the Workforce

GOAL ▶ Compare health-related careers

A There are many health-related careers that don't require a doctoral degree. Look at the list of jobs below. Which ones have you heard of? What do you think each person does?

athletic trainer	massage therapist	physical therapist
dietitian / nutritionist	occupational therapist	physical therapist assistant / aide

B Study the chart below and write the correct occupation in the first column.

Occupation	Job Summary	Education Needed	2020 Median Pay
	Prevent, diagnose, and treat muscle and bone injuries and illnesses	Bachelor's degree	$49,860
	Plan nutritional programs to help people lead healthy lives	Bachelor's degree	$63,090
	Use touch to manipulate the muscles and other soft tissues of the body	Postsecondary certificate	$43,620
	Treat patients who have injuries, illnesses, or disabilities through the therapeutic use of everyday activities	Master's degree	$86,280
	Supervised by physical therapists to help patients regain movement and manage pain after injuries or illnesses	High school diploma (aide) or Associate degree (assistant)	$49,970
	Help injured or ill people improve movement and manage pain	Doctoral or professional degree	$91,010

C SEQUENCE List the jobs in order of pay, from the lowest median pay to the highest.

1. _____

2. _____

3. _____

4. _____

5. _____

6. _____

D What education is required for each job? List the job under the correct column.

Certificate	Associate Degree	Bachelor's Degree	Master's Degree	Doctoral Degree

There is one job that you only need a high school diploma for. Which one is it?

_____

E Read each scenario and work with a partner to decide which health care professional would be best.

Example: The football team at a local university needs someone to help the athletes when they get injured. ___Athletic trainer___

1. Su Jin gained 20 pounds when she was pregnant with her daughter. She wants to learn how to eat healthier and lose the extra weight. _____

2. Danilo was in a car accident and got whiplash. _____

3. Lizetta ran a half marathon last week and her body is really sore. _____

4. Asha had a traumatic brain injury and needs to learn how to walk again.

_____

F REFLECT Which of the health careers from the table is most interesting to you? Why? Write a short paragraph.

_____

_____

_____

_____

_____

_____

_____

G Share your paragraph with a partner.

H Study the table on dietitians and nutritionists and answer the questions that follow.

QUICK FACTS
Dietitians and Nutritionists

2020 Median Pay	$63,090 per year $30.33 per hour
Typical Entry-Level Education	Bachelor's degree
Work Experience in a Related Occupation	None
On-the-Job Training	Internship / residency
Number of Jobs, 2020	73,300
Job Outlook, 2020-30	11% (faster than average)
Employment Change, 2020-30	7,800

1. What experience is needed to become a dietitian?

    a. a bachelor's degree   b. none   c. internship   d. it doesn't say

2. What is the median pay?

    a. $30.33 per year   b. $63,090 per year   c. $73,000 per year   d. it doesn't say

3. How many jobs were there in 2020?

    a. a 63,000   b. 73,300   c. 7,800   d. it doesn't say

4. Is this a growing job field?

    a. yes   b. no   c. possibly   d. it doesn't say

5. What level of education do you need?

    a. Bachelor's degree   b. Master's degree   c. Associate degree   d. it doesn't say

6. What state has the most job openings for dietitians?

    a. Texas   b. California   c. New York   d. doesn't say

I ANALYZE Work with a partner and write four reasons why this would be a good job to have.

1. _____

2. _____

3. _____

4. _____

J Share your ideas with the class.

Review

A **Match each condition with the doctor who treats it. Then use the information to practice the conversation and make new conversations.**

1. __b__ My skin is very red and itchy.
2. _____ My heart is beating quickly.
3. _____ My husband is always sneezing.
4. _____ My baby is coughing.
5. _____ My mother's toe hurts.
6. _____ There is something in my eye.
7. _____ My brother has a cavity.
8. _____ I feel nervous all the time.
9. _____ My sister is pregnant.

a. dentist
b. dermatologist
c. gynecologist / obstetrician
d. cardiologist
e. pediatrician
f. ophthalmologist
g. podiatrist
h. allergist
i. psychiatrist

Student A: My skin is very red and itchy. What should I do?

Student B: You should see a dermatologist.

B **Make sentences using the present perfect and *for* or *since*.**

1. Hugo has a backache / Monday
   Hugo has had a backache since Monday.

2. my neck hurts / two days
   _____

3. Maria feels dizzy / yesterday
   _____

4. my children have a cold / Friday
   _____

5. Pedro is sick / two weeks
   _____

6. I have an earache / 10:00 a.m.
   _____

7. they are absent from work / one month
   _____

Learner Log	I can identify parts of the body.	I can communicate symptoms.
	☐ Yes ☐ No ☐ Maybe	☐ Yes ☐ No ☐ Maybe

C **Complete each future conditional statement.**

1. If you eat out every night, _____ you will spend a lot of money _____.

2. _____ if he goes to the best doctors in the country.

3. If _____, they will look and feel great.

4. If Paulo smokes a pack of cigarettes a day, _____.

5. If _____, you will get sick.

6. If _____, you will improve your flexibility.

7. If you read nutritional labels, _____.

8. If _____, you will have a lot of cavities.

D **Read the information. Then decide if the statements below are *True* or *False*.**
Check (✓) the correct answer.

Find your balance between food and physical activity

- Be sure to stay within your daily calorie needs.
- Be physically active for at least 30 minutes most days of the week.
- About 60 minutes a day of physical activity may be needed to prevent weight gain.
- For sustaining weight loss, at least 30 minutes a day of physical activity may be required.
- Children and teenagers should be physically active for 60 minutes every day, or most days.

Know the limits on fats, sugars, and salt (sodium)

- Make the most of your fat sources from fish, nuts, and vegetable oils.
- Limit solid fats like butter, stick margarine, shortening, and lard, as well as foods that contain these.
- Check the Nutrition Facts label to keep saturated fats, trans fats, and sodium low.
- Choose food and beverages low in added sugars. Added sugars contribute calories with few, if any, nutrients.

	True	False
1. Children need to exercise for only 20 minutes a day.	☐	☐
2. Choose foods that are low in added sugar.	☐	☐
3. If you want to lose weight, you should exercise between 60 and 90 minutes a day.	☐	☐
4. Fish and nuts are good fats.	☐	☐

Learner Log   I can identify and analyze health habits.
☐ Yes ☐ No ☐ Maybe

Review

E With a partner, ask and answer questions about the nutrition information on a package of frozen peas. Decide if frozen peas are a healthy choice.

Frozen Peas Nutrition Facts	Amount/Serving	%DV*
Ingredients: green peas, salt	Total Carbohydrate 12g	4%
Serving size: 2/3 cup (88g)	Fiber 4g	16%
Servings Per Container: About 5	Sugars 6g	
	Protein 5g	
Calories 70	Vitamin A	6%
Calories from Fat 5	Vitamin C	15%
Total Fat 0.5g 1%	Calcium 0%	0%
Sat. Fat 0g 0%	Iron 4%	4%
Cholesterol 0mg 0%	*Percent Daily Values are based on a 2,000 calorie diet. Your Daily Values may be higher or lower depending on your calorie needs.	
Sodium 100mg 4%		

1. Are the peas high in fat?

2. Are the peas low in sodium?

3. Do they contain any protein? How much?

4. What vitamins do they contain? Are they high in vitamins?

5. Are the peas a good source of calcium?

6. Do you think peas are a healthy food choice?

F Look back at the article in **D** on page 139. Write two pieces of advice that you would like to follow.

1. _____

2. _____

G Make a chart in your notebook. Put each word into the correct category. Use a dictionary to check your answers.

active	cough	gain	hospital	~~ophthalmologist~~	sore	stretch
ankle	dentist	gentle	~~itchy~~	protect	stay	tired
cholesterol	diabetes	healthy	maintain	raw	stress	~~worry~~

Noun	Verb	Adjective
ophthalmologist	worry	itchy

Learner Log	I can analyze nutrition information. ☐ Yes ☐ No ☐ Maybe	I can interpret fitness information. ☐ Yes ☐ No ☐ Maybe

Create a Healthy-Living Plan

SOFT SKILL ▶ Collaboration

You are a team of doctors and health-care professionals who have decided to make a healthy-living plan to give patients when they leave the hospital.

1. Form a team of four or five students. Choose a position for each member of your team.

Position	Job Description	Student Name
Student 1: Health Advisor	Check that everyone speaks English. Check that everyone participates.	
Student 2: Writer	Write down information for the plan with the help of your team.	
Student 3: Designer	Design plan layout and add artwork.	
Students 4/5: Health Representatives	Help writer and designer with their work.	

2. Make a list of all the information you want to include in your plan (healthy habits, fitness and nutrition advice, etc.).

3. Create the different sections of your plan, for example, a guide to reading nutritional labels, a guide to exercise, a list of doctors and their specializations, and a guide to common symptoms and diseases.

4. Add artwork to the plan, for example, maps of parks and gyms in your area, or a drawing of the food pyramid.

5. Make a collage of all your information.

6. Share your healthy-living plan with the class.

Collaboration:
Express disagreements politely
It is important to make your voice heard when in a group discussion, but be polite. Look at the examples below:

"I think it would be better if we put _____ in our plan."

"Maybe we should reconsider putting _____ in our plan. How about _____ instead?"

Some people try to eat locally grown food to stay healthy and help their community.

Reading Challenge

A PREDICT Look at the photo. What is the man doing? How old do you think he is?

B Look at the list. Discuss which items are the most important for living a long life.

- being active
- spending time with family and friends
- living alone in a city
- having a sense of humor
- eating healthy food
- retiring early

C You are going to read about *blue zones*. There are five places in the world considered blue zones. Write them on the map below.

- Ikari, Greece
- Loma Linda, USA
- Nicoya, Costa Rica
- Okinawa, Japan
- Sardinia, Italy

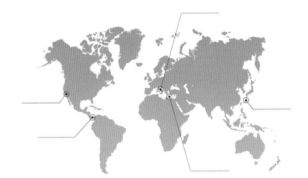

D Read about blue zones.

E ANALYZE Discuss the vocabulary below. Which words in the text are positive? Which words are negative? Which words are neither positive nor negative? Why?

Alzheimer's	elders	locally grown
celebrated	isolated	reduce stress
disease	laughter	

F What does the reading NOT list as a reason that Sardinians live so long?

a. Sardinia is an isolated island.

b. Elders are celebrated.

c. Physical activity is a way of life.

d. Many of them have heart disease and Alzheimer's.

G Life expectancy is how long people are expected to live. What blue zone principles raised the life expectancy in Minnesota? Discuss and make a list on a separate piece of paper.

Blue Zones 🔊

What would you say if someone told you that by making a few changes in your life, you could live longer and spend less time at the doctor's office? Chances are, if you live in a blue zone, you already live this life. Blue zones are areas in the world where people live longer and have almost no chronic diseases like cancer, obesity or dementia.

5　　One blue zone is Sardinia, Italy. Sardinians live longer than most people. In fact, Sardinia has ten times more centenarians (people who have lived to 100 years old) than the United States. One of the reasons for this is that Sardinia is a very <u>isolated</u> island. In addition, Sardinians are culturally isolated as well. This has led to a very traditional lifestyle: family is important, their food is locally grown, and physical

10　activity is a part of daily life. Today, they hunt, fish, and harvest their food in the same way they have always done. They eat a diet high in omega-3 fatty acids, which possibly helps protect them from heart disease and Alzheimer's.* They are very close with their family and friends, and social gatherings are important. Elders are always celebrated and laughter helps reduce their stress. They use their legs for

15　transportation and their bodies for physical labor, keeping them physically fit. All of these lifestyle characteristics are why the island of Sardinia is considered a blue zone.

　　In 2009, they tested the blue zone principles in a mid-western city, Albert Lea, Minnesota. The residents there learned how to move more, eat better, connect with one another and have a positive outlook. The results? The life expectancy increased

20　by three years and this lowered health care costs by almost 40%. Could something like this happen in your community? There's only one way to find out!

　　Think about it: if you follow these lifestyle characteristics yourself, you will live longer!

Alzheimer's a disease that leads to memory loss

6 Getting Hired

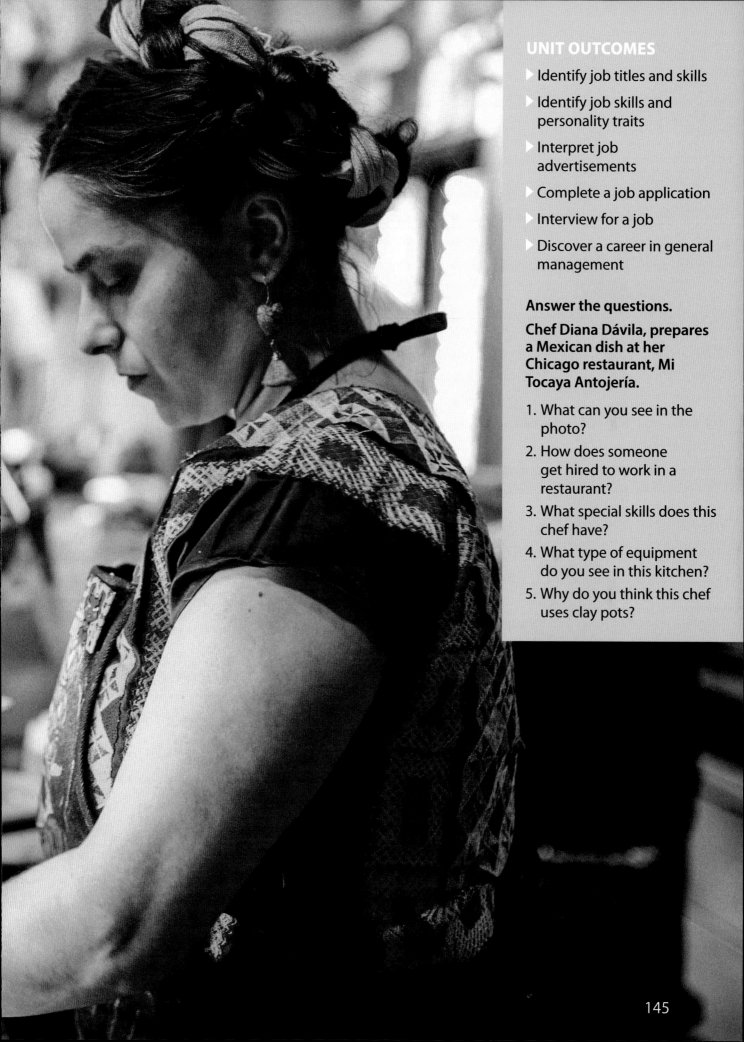

▶ Identify job titles and skills

▶ Identify job skills and personality traits

▶ Interpret job advertisements

▶ Complete a job application

▶ Interview for a job

▶ Discover a career in general management

Answer the questions.

Chef Diana Dávila, prepares a Mexican dish at her Chicago restaurant, Mi Tocaya Antojería.

1. What can you see in the photo?
2. How does someone get hired to work in a restaurant?
3. What special skills does this chef have?
4. What type of equipment do you see in this kitchen?
5. Why do you think this chef uses clay pots?

145

Jobs and Careers

GOAL ▶ Identify job titles and skills

A **Look at the photos and write the correct letter for each job.**

a.

b.

c.

d.

Job	Letter
graphic designer	_c_
dental hygienist	_____
home health aide	_____
accountant	_____

B **ANALYZE Talk to your partner about the four jobs in A. Which job is the most interesting? Which job is the most difficult? Why?**

C Match the job with the description.

_____ 1. graphic designer   a. cleans teeth

_____ 2. repair technician   b. takes care of children

_____ 3. administrative assistant c. designs and maintains yards

_____ 4. dental hygienist   d. supervises internet security

_____ 5. landscaper   e. designs artwork for companies

_____ 6. accountant   f. does general office work

_____ 7. home health aide   g. uses equipment in a factory or on a construction site

_____ 8. cyber security specialist h. keeps financial records

_____ 9. nanny   i. fixes appliances and equipment

_____ 10. machine operator   j. takes care of sick people in their own homes

D Look at the pictures. What do you think each person does? Write a job title.

cyber security specialist	judge	physical therapist	server
doctor	~~lawyer~~	plumber	teacher

1. _____lawyer_____

2. _____

3. _____

4. _____

5. _____

6. _____

7. _____

8. _____

E IDENTIFY Work in a small group to write one skill for each job title.

1. doctor _____

2. server _____

3. cyber security specialist _____

4. postal worker _____

F Work in a small group again to write the job title for each skill.

1. _____ fixes leaking pipes

2. _____ helps children learn

3. _____ delivers mail and packages

4. _____ works for a client in matters of the law

Simple Present

The simple present is used to talk about things that are routine or always true.

G Practice the conversation with a partner. Use the job titles and skills from this lesson to make new conversations.

Student A: What does a graphic designer do?

Student B: A graphic designer makes artwork for companies.

H Work with a partner. Think of more jobs and write what each person does.

1. A farmer grows fruits and vegetables. _____

2. _____

3. _____

4. _____

I When searching for information online, you want to ask _____ a clear question or type in key words. Read the question below and underline the key words.

Life ONLINE

What skills do you need to be an electrician?

Now write your own question and key words that you would type into a search engine about a job you are interested in.

Question: _____

Key words: _____

What Can You Do?

GOAL ▶ Identify job skills and personality traits

A EVALUATE What are your job skills? Check (✓) the things you are good at. Add two skills to the list.

- ☐ manage schedules
- ☐ assemble things
- ☐ cook
- ☐ draw
- ☐ drive a car or truck
- ☐ fix machines
- ☐ order supplies
- ☐ balance accounts
- ☐ operate machines
- ☐ talk to customers

- ☐ communicate clearly
- ☐ sew
- ☐ speak other languages
- ☐ take care of children
- ☐ take care of the elderly
- ☐ type
- ☐ repair computers
- ☐ manage social media accounts
- ☐ _____
- ☐ _____

B Write two skills you want to improve and two skills you want to learn.

Skills I Want to Improve	Skills I Want to Learn

C Work with a partner. Think of ways your partner can learn or improve the skills he or she wrote in B. Use ideas from the box and make suggestions for your partner.

ask a friend to teach you	practice at home	take an online class
do training at your company	take an evening class	volunteer

Student A: I want to learn how to <u>take care of the elderly</u>.

Student B: Maybe you could <u>volunteer at a hospital or nursing home</u>.

D **SUGGEST** Claude needs a job. Can you suggest two for him? 🎧

Claude is quiet and shy. He is friendly, but he doesn't really like to talk to customers. He is very good at assembling things. When he was a teenager, he enjoyed fixing bicycles. He likes to be busy. He wants to get a job where he can use his technical skills.

1. _____

2. _____

E Study the chart with your classmates and teacher. Then underline examples of infinitives and gerunds in the paragraph in **D**.

Infinitives and Gerunds Infinitive = to + Verb Gerund = Verb + *ing*			
Verb	**Infinitive or Gerund**	**Example Sentence**	**Other Verbs That Follow the Same Rule**
want	infinitive	He wants **to get** a job.	plan, decide
enjoy	gerund	He enjoys **fixing** bicycles.	finish, give up
like	both	He likes **to talk.** He likes **talking.**	love, hate
Some verbs take the infinitive and some verbs take the gerund. There are some verbs that take both.			

F Are these verbs followed by an infinitive, a gerund, or both? Check (✓) the correct answers.

1. I like _____ on a team. ☐ to work ☐ working ☐ to work / working

2. I enjoy _____ problems. ☐ to solve ☐ solving ☐ to solve / solving

3. I want _____ to customers. ☐ to talk ☐ talking ☐ to talk / talking

4. I decided _____ math. ☐ to study ☐ studying ☐ to study / studying

5. I hate _____ decisions. ☐ to make ☐ making ☐ to make / making

6. I gave up _____ two years ago. ☐ to smoke ☐ smoking ☐ to smoke / smoking

7. I love _____ machines. ☐ to fix ☐ fixing ☐ to fix / fixing

G **EVALUATE** What kind of personal skills do you have? Check (✓) the ones that describe you and add more skills to the list.

☐ solve problems

☐ work under pressure

☐ work in a fast-paced environment

☐ work on a team

☐ make decisions

☐ pay attention to details

☐ work with my hands

☐ read and follow directions

☐ help people

☐ organize information

☐ work with money

☐ talk to customers

☐ _____

☐ _____

☐ _____

☐ _____

H Study the chart with your classmates and teacher.

			Gerunds and Nouns after Prepositions		
Subject	**Verb**	**Adjective**	**Preposition**	**Gerund / Noun**	**Example Sentence**
I	am	good	at	fixing bicycles.	I am good at **fixing bicycles.**
She	is	good	at	math.	She is good at **math.**
A gerund or a noun follows an adjective + a preposition. Some other examples of adjectives + prepositions are *interested in, afraid of, tired of, bad at,* and *worried about.* When a noun is plural, it is also common to use the preposition *with: I am good with customers.*					

I Tell your partner about your skills and interests. What things are you *good at, bad at, interested in, tired of,* and *afraid of*? Your partner will suggest a good job for you.

EXAMPLE: **Student A:** I'm good at <u>paying attention to details</u>. I'm interested in <u>organizing information</u>.

Student B: Maybe you should be <u>an accountant</u>.

J **APPLY** Write a paragraph about your job skills. Describe the job skills you have or are interested in learning. Say why these skills are important and useful.

_____

_____

_____

_____

_____

Help Wanted

GOAL ▶ Interpret job advertisements

A **Read the following job advertisements.**

1. AUTO TECHNICIAN

Job Type: PT

Do you like to work on cars? Do you have an excellent attitude, good mechanical skills, and the ability to learn fast? Strong electronics background preferred. Call Kip Jones at (310) 555-9078 or email resume to kjones@j0ne5aut0m0tive.com

APPLY NOW

2. ADMINISTRATIVE ASSISTANT

Job Type: FT 40K–45K / year

Acme Construction. Minimum two years' experience. Good computer skills required (Word, Excel, manage social media accounts). Must be good at working under pressure. Email: jobs@acm3.com

APPLY NOW

3. RECEPTIONIST

Job Type: PT (weekends: 10 a.m.–6 p.m.)

HS diploma (or equivalent) and one year's experience. Excellent phone and organizational skills along with a pleasant attitude are a must! Please apply in person at: 396 Marcasel Avenue, Los Angeles, CA 90066

APPLY NOW

4. MEAT AND PRODUCE MANAGERS

Job Type: FT

Fast-growing supermarket chain seeks bright and motivated managers for meat and produce sections. Prior management experience required. Excellent salary and benefits. Call: (626) 555-1342

APPLY NOW

5. PHARMACY CLERK

Job Type: PT

Detail-oriented pharmacy clerk needed to process insurance forms and assist customers. Must be bilingual (English and Spanish). Must have strong communication and organizational skills. Great benefits. Call Armine: (626) 555-6613

APPLY NOW

6. CUSTODIAN

Job Type: FT $14–16 / hr + benefits

Dependable custodian for three apartment buildings. Minimum two years' experience in plumbing, carpentry, painting, and repairs. Must have own tools and car. Call: (818) 555-3500 ext. 523

APPLY NOW

B **Are there any words or abbreviations that are new to you? List them below and discuss them with your classmates and teacher.**

_____ _____ _____

_____ _____ _____

_____ _____ _____

C **INTERPRET** **Read the ads in A again and answer the questions below.**

1. What experience should the auto technician have? _____ *electronics background* _____

2. Which employer wants someone who can work under pressure? _____

3. Which job requires a friendly personality? _____

4. Which job requires a car? _____

5. Which job requires someone who is detail-oriented? _____

6. Which job requires someone who is bilingual? _____

7. What are ways to apply for these jobs? _____

D **What skills are required for each job advertised in A? Complete the table.**

Job	Skills Required or Preferred
auto technician	
administrative assistant	
receptionist	
meat and produce managers	
pharmacy clerk	
custodian	

E **Read the descriptions and decide which job or jobs from A each person should apply for. Write the job titles.**

1. Addisu recently moved here and needs to find a job. At his old job, he answered the phone, scheduled meetings, and sent memos. He would like a job doing the same thing. Which job or jobs should he apply for?

_____

2. Kyung was recently laid off from his janitorial job at the local school district. He had been working there for ten years and took care of all the maintenance and repairs for the school. Which job or jobs should he apply for?

_____

3. Hayma wants to find some extra work on the weekends. She is good at answering phones and she is very organized. Which job or jobs should she apply for?

_____

4. Rita manages a bakery but wants to find a job closer to home. She is smart and willing to work hard. She really likes to work with people and would like to find a job in the same line of work. Which job or jobs should she apply for?

_____

F **REFLECT Answer the following questions about yourself.**

1. Which job advertised in **A** is best for you? Why?

_____

2. Which job would you most like to have? Why?

_____

3. Which job would you like the least? Why?

_____

G **CREATE On a separate piece of paper, write an ad for your dream job. Include the job title, skills, preferences, pay, and any other necessary information.**

Employment History

GOAL ▶ Complete a job application

A **Look at the ways people apply for jobs. How did you get your last job? What's the best way to get a job? Discuss your answers with a partner.**

- know someone at a company (personal connection)
- go to an employment agency
- join a professional network
- see a *Help Wanted* sign and fill out an application
- introduce yourself to the manager and fill out an application
- send a resume to a company

Life
ONLINE

Joining professional social media sites is very useful. You can set the parameters of what type of job you are looking for, have alerts sent to you, and get recommendations there.

B **Not every business advertises available positions. If you want to work somewhere, you should go in and ask for an application. Read the conversation below.**

Ramona: Excuse me. May I speak to the manager, please?

Employee: She's not here right now. Can I help you?

Ramona: Are you hiring?

Employee: As a matter of fact, we are.

Ramona: What positions are you hiring for?

Employee: We need a <u>manicurist</u> and a <u>receptionist</u>.

Ramona: Great. Can I have an application, please?

Employee: Here you go. You can drop it off any time.

Ramona: Thanks a lot.

Employee: Sure. Good luck.

C **Practice the conversation in B. Use the job titles from this unit to make new conversations.**

D **On a job application, you have to fill in certain information. Match the type of information to its description.**

_c_ 1. Personal information

_____ 2. Employment history

_____ 3. Availability

_____ 4. Education

_____ 5. References

a. people you have worked with

b. previous jobs you have had

c. name, address, skills

d. schools you attended

e. when you are free to work

E ANALYZE Look at Ramona's online job application. Think about how you would fill it out for yourself.

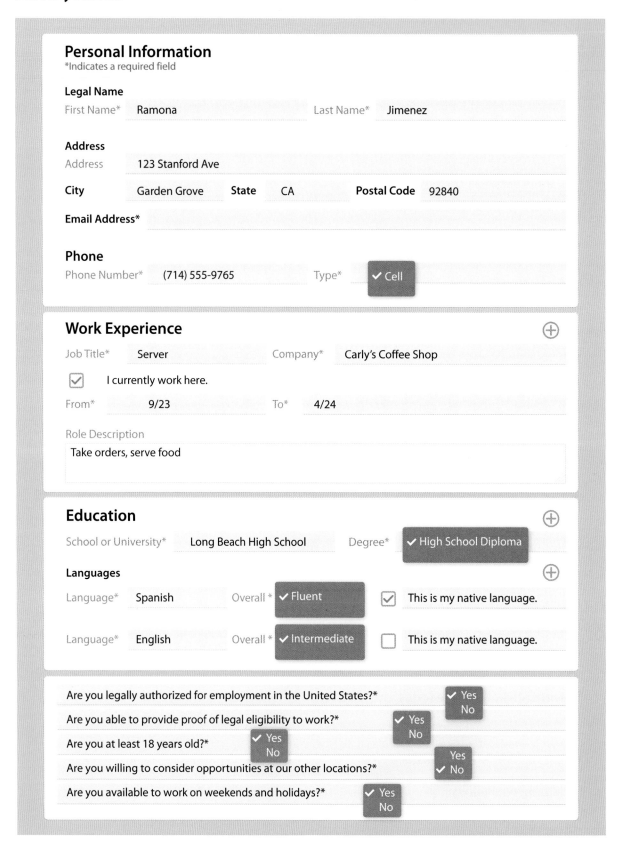

Personal Information
*Indicates a required field

Legal Name

First Name* Ramona   Last Name* Jimenez

Address

Address   123 Stanford Ave

City   Garden Grove   State   CA   Postal Code   92840

Email Address*

Phone

Phone Number*   (714) 555-9765   Type*   ✔ Cell

Work Experience ⊕

Job Title*   Server   Company*   Carly's Coffee Shop

☑   I currently work here.

From*   9/23   To*   4/24

Role Description

Take orders, serve food

Education ⊕

School or University*   Long Beach High School   Degree*   ✔ High School Diploma

Languages ⊕

Language*   Spanish   Overall *   ✔ Fluent   ☑   This is my native language.

Language*   English   Overall *   ✔ Intermediate   ☐   This is my native language.

Are you legally authorized for employment in the United States?*   ✔ Yes / No

Are you able to provide proof of legal eligibility to work?*   ✔ Yes / No

Are you at least 18 years old?*   ✔ Yes / No

Are you willing to consider opportunities at our other locations?*   Yes / ✔ No

Are you available to work on weekends and holidays?*   ✔ Yes / No

F **APPLY** Complete this online application form. Circle your answer in the drop-down menus.

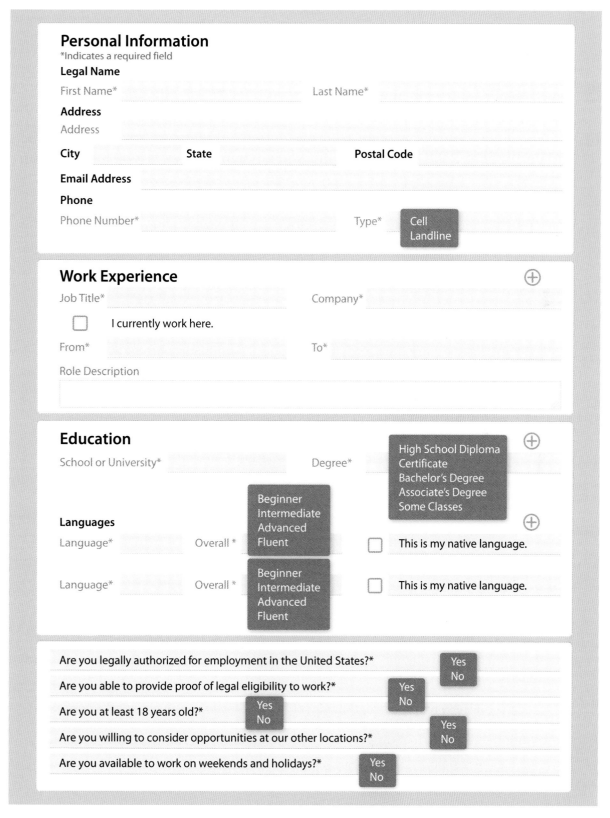

Personal Information
*Indicates a required field

Legal Name

First Name*　　　　　　　　　　　　　Last Name*

Address

Address

City　　　　**State**　　　　**Postal Code**

Email Address

Phone

Phone Number*　　　　　　　　Type*　　Cell
　　　　　　　　　　　　　　　　　　　Landline

Work Experience ⊕

Job Title*　　　　　　　　　　Company*

☐　I currently work here.

From*　　　　　　　　　　To*

Role Description

Education ⊕

School or University*　　　　Degree*　　High School Diploma
　　　　　　　　　　　　　　　　　　Certificate
　　　　　　　　　　　　　　　　　　Bachelor's Degree
　　　　　　　　　　　　　　　　　　Associate's Degree
　　　　　　　　　　　　　　　　　　Some Classes

Languages ⊕

Language*　　Overall *　Beginner　　☐　This is my native language.
　　　　　　　　　　　Intermediate
　　　　　　　　　　　Advanced
　　　　　　　　　　　Fluent

Language*　　Overall *　Beginner　　☐　This is my native language.
　　　　　　　　　　　Intermediate
　　　　　　　　　　　Advanced
　　　　　　　　　　　Fluent

Are you legally authorized for employment in the United States?*　　Yes / No

Are you able to provide proof of legal eligibility to work?*　　Yes / No

Are you at least 18 years old?*　　Yes / No

Are you willing to consider opportunities at our other locations?*　　Yes / No

Are you available to work on weekends and holidays?*　　Yes / No

G Think of three companies you could apply to work at. Go online and practice filling out an application.

Why Do You Want to Work Here?

GOAL ▶ Interview for a job

A Have you ever had a job interview? What happened? Tell your partner.

B During a job interview, an employer tries to find out about an applicant's character and personality. Read and listen to find out what interviewers look for during an interview. 🎧

Your job interview is the most important part of the application process. This is when the employer gets to meet you and learn more about you. Employers are interested in your skills and experience, but they also look for personality and character traits.

Do you stand tall and smile confidently? Employers will notice your self-confidence. Managers want to hire employees who have confidence in themselves and will have confidence in the job they are doing.

Do you like to work hard and do a good job? Another important thing an interviewer looks for is enthusiasm about work. People who are enthusiastic about a job make great employees. They are happy with the work and usually stay with the company for a while.

Are you friendly and easy to talk to? Do you pay attention to how other people are feeling? Warmth and sensitivity are also very important traits. A person with these characteristics will make a good coworker; someone who can work well with others.

Do you have some or all of these traits? Can you show that you have these traits in an interview? If the answer is yes, you will have a good chance of getting the job.

C **EXPLAIN** Discuss the following questions with a partner.

1. In your opinion, which is the most important trait: self-confidence, enthusiasm, or a friendly personality?

2. According to the information in **B**, how can you use body language to show you are self-confident? Can you think of any other ways you can show confidence through body language?

3. How can you show an employer that you are enthusiastic about a job and a company?

4. According to the information, why do employers like to hire warm, sensitive people?

5. Do you think there are other character traits that employers like? What are they?

D Imagine you are interviewing someone for a job as an administrative assistant in a busy doctor's office. List six personality traits you would look for.

arrogant	confident	friendly	helpful	intelligent	sensitive	thoughtful
careful	enthusiastic	funny	honest	motivated	sneaky	warm

1. _____   2. _____   3. _____

4. _____   5. _____   6. _____

E **DETERMINE** Discuss what clothing and accessories are appropriate or not appropriate for a job interview. Fill in the chart with your ideas.

Men	
Appropriate	**Not Appropriate**
long-sleeved shirt	t-shirt

Women	
Appropriate	**Not Appropriate**
	t-shirt

F Study the chart with your classmates and teacher.

Would rather					
Subject	*Would rather*	**Base Form**	*than*	**Base Form**	**Example Sentence**
I / You / She / He / It / We / They	would ('d) rather	work alone	than	work with people.	I **would rather** work alone **than** work with people.
Note: You can omit the second verb if it is the same as the first verb: *I would rather work nights than (work) days.*					

G Which work situation do you prefer? Talk to your partner about your preferences.

EXAMPLE: **Student A:** Would you rather work inside or outside?

              Student B: I'd rather work inside because I hate the cold.

1. work alone / on a team   **2.** work days / nights

3. get paid hourly / weekly   **4.** have your own business / work for someone else

5. retire at 65 / work until you are 70   **6.** walk to work / drive to work

H Write sentences about your ideal work situation.

1. _I'd rather work on a team than alone because I like talking to people._____

2. _____

3. _____

I PREPARE Imagine you are preparing for a job interview. Choose a job from the ads on page 152 or one of your own. Work with a partner and answer the questions below.

1. What are your skills?

2. Why do you think you would be good at this job?

3. How would you describe your personality?

4. What did you like and dislike about your last job?

5. Would you rather work full-time or part-time?

6. What salary do you expect?

LESSON 6

Explore the Workforce

GOAL ▶ Discover a career in general management

A **What does a general manager do? Write a brief description with a partner.**

A general manager _____

_____

B **Look at the statistics below and ask and answer questions with a partner.**

General Managers
in the US
974,878

Gender
Male 71%
Female 29%

Average Age
44

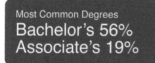

Most Common Degrees
Bachelor's 56%
Associate's 19%

1. What is the average age of a general manager?

2. How many general managers are there in the US?

3. What is the most common degree for a general manager?

4. Is it more common for a general manager to be male or female?

C **Look at the statistics below. Using the information above, fill in the some of the missing words. Guess the rest. Then listen and confirm your answers.** 🎧

1. General managers are paid an average annual _____ of $65,517.

2. 29% of all general managers are _____, while 71% are

   _____.

3. The average age of a working general manager is _____ years old.

4. The large number of general managers live in _____ and
   _____.

5. A general manager's average _____ is $36,000.

6. New York, NY, pays an annual average wage of _____, the highest in
   the US.

7. _____ is the best state for general managers to live.

8. General managers are most needed in _____.

D **INFER** Discuss and write answers with a small group.

1. Look at numbers 1 and 5 in **C**. What is the difference between an average annual salary and a starting salary?

   _____

   _____

2. Look at numbers 7 and 8. What is the difference between these two statements?

   _____

   _____

3. Why do you think more men than women are general managers?

   _____

   _____

E **Study the data in the chart. Use it to fill the pie chart legend.**

General Manager Race	Percentage
American Indian and Alaska Native	0.6%
Asian	6.1%
Black or African American	6.0%
Hispanic or Latino	14.3%
Unknown	2.1%
White	70.9%

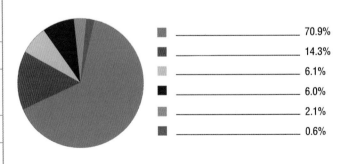

Based on your race AND where you live, do you have a good chance of getting a job as general manager? Why or why not? _____

_____

F **ASSESS** What skills are needed to be a good general manager? Circle the skills below. Then check (✓) the skills you have.

☐ Communication skills   ☐ Leadership skills   ☐ Organizational skills

☐ Problem solving   ☐ Critical thinking   ☐ Technical skills

G **ANALYZE** Read the job ad and circle the parts that describe you.

General Manager

Silver Sneakers Gym Fort Worth, TX   **$70,000 to 100,000 annually**

Do you want to work in an environment with great people, have great benefits, paid time off, free gym membership and opportunities to learn to grow within a company?

We are looking for talented individuals who:
- Have a positive, upbeat, and outgoing attitude
- Are passionate about hospitality and excellence for our members
- Have fitness industry experience (preferred)
- Love to constantly learn and grow

There are some MUST HAVES:
- 3-5 years of management experience supervising 3-10 employees in a team environment, with measurable outcomes of employee development and promotion
- Success in creating new teams and / or rebuilding teams in a collaborative environment
- Excellent communication skills, oral and written, with a heavy emphasis on listening!
- A high school diploma or equivalent is required and gets you in the door, but we'd love to see a bachelor's degree
- Cardiopulmonary Resuscitation (CPR) and Automated External Defibrillator (AED) certification required

Note: This job requires the ability to move and lift up to 25 lbs. Standing, sitting, or walking for extended periods of time and appearance in a clean uniform are also required.

H **REFLECT** Is this a job you would like to have? Why or why not?

I **Go online and find a job advertisement for a sales manager. Answer the following questions.**

1. What is the job title?   4. What is the salary range?

2. Where is the job located?   5. What experience is needed?

3. Is it full time or part-time?

Review

A **Read each skill below and write the correct job title on the line.**

1. cleans teeth _____

2. send memos, files, and does general office work _____

3. takes a patient's temperature and blood pressure _____

4. fixes pipes _____

5. maintains office buildings _____

6. uses equipment in a factory or a construction site _____

7. takes care of children _____

8. maintains yards _____

B **List six job skills you have.**

1. _____

2. _____

3. _____

4. _____

5. _____

6. _____

C **Complete the sentences using the gerund or infinitive form of the verb in parentheses.**

1. I like _____ on a team. (work)

2. I am good at _____ to customers. (talk)

3. They hate _____ the phone. (answer)

4. I decided _____ a computer course next semester. (study)

5. He is interested in _____ cars. (repair)

6. We finished _____ our reports yesterday. (write)

Learner Log	I can identify job titles and skills. ☐ Yes ☐ No ☐ Maybe	I can identify job skills and personality traits. ☐ Yes ☐ No ☐ Maybe

D **Read the job ads.**

1. **ADMINISTRATIVE ASSISTANT**

FT: 10 a.m. – 6 p.m.
Requires HS diploma and one-year's experience.
Excellent phone, computer, and organizational
skills along with a pleasant attitude is a must!
Please send resume to: jobs@aaj08s.com

APPLY NOW

2. **CUSTODIAN**

Reliable custodian for local school district.
Minimum one-year's experience cleaning,
plumbing, carpentry, painting, and repairs.
Will provide supplies and tools.
$14–16 / hr + benefits
Call: (818) 555-6879

APPLY NOW

E **Look at the ads in D. Write:** *administrative assistant, custodian,* **or** *both.*

1. Which job requires experience?

2. Which job offers benefits?

3. Which job requires a high school diploma?

4. Personality is NOT important for which job?

F **Fill out the partial online job application.**

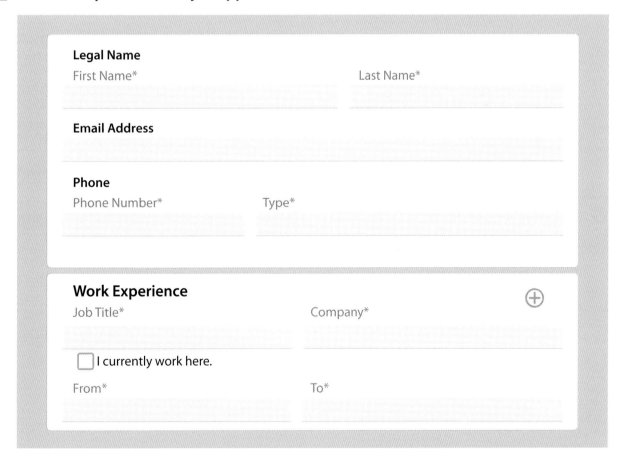

Legal Name

First Name*

Last Name*

Email Address

Phone

Phone Number*

Type*

Work Experience ⊕

Job Title*

Company*

☐ I currently work here.

From*

To*

Learner Log   I can interpret job advertisements.
　　　　　　　　☐ Yes　☐ No　☐ Maybe

I can complete a job application.
☐ Yes　☐ No　☐ Maybe

Review

G **What kind of personality traits should people have for these jobs? Write two adjectives for each job. Share your answers with a partner.**

1. home health aide: _responsible, caring_

2. manager in a clothing store: _____

3. receptionist in a dentist's office: _____

4. hair dresser: _____

5. sales representative: _____

6. teacher: _____

H **Write six interview questions for one of the following jobs. Interview a partner.**

assembler in a factory	computer technician	home health aide	receptionist
bookkeeper	furniture store manager	landscaper	waiter

1. _____

2. _____

3. _____

4. _____

5. _____

6. _____

I **Dictionaries use different symbols to show word stress. Look up the following words in the dictionary. Write them with the correct syllable stress.**

1. applicant _ap'-pli-cant_

2. previous _____

3. bookkeeper _____

4. technician _____

5. computer _____

6. equipment _____

7. environment _____

8. require _____

Learner Log	I can interview for a job.
	☐ Yes ☐ No ☐ Maybe

Create a Job Ad for a Job Fair
SOFT SKILL ▶ Collaboration

With your team, you will come up with a job ad and write a complete description of what you are looking for. Then you will present your job ad at the job fair.

1. Form a hiring committee of four or five students. Choose a position for each member of your committee.

Position	Job Description	Student Name
Student 1: Chair	Check that everyone speaks English and works on their tasks.	
Student 2: Secretary	Takes notes during the brainstorming session.	
Student 3: Designer	Designs job advertisement with help from the group.	
Student 4: Recruiter	Shares job advertisement at the job fair.	
Student 5: Member	Help secretary and designer with their work.	

2. **DECIDE** Choose a job that you would like to write a job description for.

3. **COLLABORATE** Work as a team to come up with a job title, job details (hours, pay, etc.) and requirements (experience, skills, education, languages, etc.). This should be a very detailed list of everything you want in an employee.

4. Take the information you've gathered and write a job advertisement (see examples in Lesson 3 and Review). Create an online version of the advertisement.

5. Share your advertisement at the job fair in your classroom.

 Life ONLINE Use a shared doc to brainstorm. If everyone has access, you can type your ideas, and everyone will be able to see them.

COLLABORATION:
Brainstorm Ideas
There are different ways to brainstorm ideas.
1. Have everyone quietly write down their ideas on a piece of paper and then share.
2. Go around the group and one by one, each person / member adds an idea to the mix.
3. Students call out ideas as they come to them. Make sure that one person is writing all the ideas down.

Job Fair
A place where you go to see what jobs are available in your community. Companies will come to advertise their job, and you may even get to fill out an application and have an interview on the spot!

Reading Challenge

A **Study the table and answer the questions that follow.**

Bureau of Labor Statistics (bls.gov) Annual Mean Wages in 2019	
Trade	Wages
Brick masons and block masons	$56,470
Carpenters	$52,850
Electricians	$60,370
Fitness instructors	$45,110
Plumbers	$55,160

1. What does each person do?

2. Which trades make the most money? The least?

B **Read the text.**

C **INFER Choose the best answer.**

1. In line 11, what do you think *job security* means?

   a. a job that is hard to find

   b. a job as a security officer

   c. a job that many people have

   d. a job that is secure, one that you can do for a long time

2. In line 11, what do you think *growth rate* means?

   a. how much something grows from one time period to the next

   b. a company that grows quickly

   c. a company that doesn't grow

3. According to the reading, which job should be the easiest to get?

   a. electrician

   b. solar panel installer

   c. plumber

   d. carpenter

D **REFLECT Look at the photo. Is the woman enjoying learning the welding trade? What trade would you like to learn? Choose a trade and write a short paragraph about why you would like to do this for a job.**

Should You Learn a Trade? 🎧

When the COVID pandemic hit in 2020, many people lost their jobs. Some industries never recovered. So, what did people do who needed to find a new line of work? Many people learned a trade, a job that requires a particular skill but no formal education, such as a plumber, an electrician, a brick mason, or a construction worker. There are many benefits to picking up a trade.

5   First, some trades will pay you as an apprentice. This means they will teach you how to do the job and pay you at the same time. For example, you could earn $20.92 an hour while you apprentice with an electrician. Or you could be an apprentice bricklayer and earn $16.02 per hour. Another benefit of learning a trade is you can enter the working world faster. Many people end up spending a lot of money to go to school and have a hard time finding a job

10 when they are ready. But if you chose to do a trade, you can work and make money right away.

    Also, there is job security in trades. In the next 10 years, the average growth rate for most jobs is 4%. However, jobs for electricians are expected to increase 8% nationwide from 2019-2029 and jobs for solar panel installers are expected to increase 51% over that same time! Finally, a great benefit to learning a trade is that one day, you can own your own business.

15 Instead of working for a large company, many tradespeople work alone or with a few other people. The best part is that you have a choice.

    Learning a trade can open so many doors. You will know how to do something that many people don't. And you will be able to make money doing it for the rest of your life.

This female welder enjoys the challenges of her job.

▶ Compare employee behavior and attitudes

▶ Interpret a pay stub

▶ Analyze benefit information

▶ Identify safe workplace behavior

▶ Communicate at work

▶ Discover human resources jobs

Answer the questions.

Cynthia Gordy Giwa with Cindy Morris, the owner of Camera Ready Cutz, a barbershop in the Bedford-Stuyvesant neighborhood of Brooklyn, New York.

1. What kind of work do these people do?

2. Describe what you see in the photo.

3. What do you think are the roles of the two people in the photo?

4. What safety precautions do you think these workers need to consider?

Attitudes at Work

GOAL ▶ Compare employee behavior and attitudes

A Listen to two employees talk about their jobs. What does Leticia do? What does So do? 🎧

B **COMPARE** With a partner, write examples of the two employees' behavior in the table.

Leticia	So
comes to work on time	

C **ANALYZE** In your opinion, who is the better employee? Why? Can you think of other examples of good and bad employee behavior? Add them to the table.

D **Read the conversation. Look at the words in *italics*. Which are possessive adjectives and which are possessive pronouns?**

Ellen: *My* boss is quite demanding and she always wants *her* reports on time.

Leticia: *Your* manager is more demanding than *mine*.

Ellen: Yes, but *yours* is less friendly.

E **Study the chart. Which possessive pronouns have an -*s* at the end? Which possessive adjectives and possessive pronouns are the same?**

Review: Possessive Adjectives and Possessive Pronouns			
Possessive Adjectives	**Rule**		
my / your / his / her / its our / their	Possessive adjectives show possession of an object and come before the noun.		
Example Sentence			
Subject	**Verb**	**Possessive Adjective**	**Object**
This	is	**her**	office.
Possessive Pronouns	**Rule**		
mine / yours / his / hers / ours / theirs	Possessive pronouns show possession of an object and act as a noun.		
Example Sentence			
Subject	**Noun**	**Verb**	**Possessive Pronoun**
This	office	is	**hers.**

F **Underline the possessive adjective(s) in each sentence. Circle the possessive pronoun.**

1. My sister's manager is generous, but my manager is more generous than hers.

2. Their job is boring, but our job is more boring than theirs.

3. My husband gets a good salary. His salary is better than mine.

4. My brother says his coworkers are friendly, but my coworkers are friendlier than his.

5. I like her manager, but mine is much more easygoing.

6. His office is clean, but ours is bigger.

G **Circle the correct word in each sentence.**

1. She keeps (her / hers) work space very clean.

2. She never eats at (her / hers) desk, but they always eat at (they / theirs).

3. That office is (you / yours).

4. (Theirs / Their) company has more employees than his.

5. That's (your / yours) book. Where is (my / mine)?

6. We will give you (our / ours) plan so you can compare it with (your / yours).

H **Read the conversation between Leticia and Ellen.**

Leticia: I think an ideal manager should be demanding.

Ellen: I agree. A manager shouldn't be too easygoing.

I **ANALYZE** **What is an ideal manager like? What are ideal coworkers like? Use the adjectives from the box and have a conversation with your partner. Can you think of more adjectives?**

ambitious	demanding	funny	interesting	quiet	serious
courteous	friendly	hardworking	patient	respectful	strict

J **In a small group, talk about your current job or previous jobs. Using possessive pronouns, write five sentences describing the experiences of your group members.**

1. Anita has a friendly manager, but Jun's manager is friendlier than hers.

2. _____

3. _____

4. _____

5. _____

6. _____

It's Pay Day!

GOAL ▶ Interpret a pay stub

A Discuss the following vocabulary with your classmates and teacher.

earnings	Medicare	social security
employee ID	net pay	state disability
federal income tax	pay period	withholdings
gross pay	pre-tax deductions	year-to-date (YTD)
401K	rate of pay	

B Look at Leticia's pay stub. Find the vocabulary from the box in **A**.

SECTION 1: PERSONAL INFORMATION

Employee Name: Leticia Rosales **Check Number:** 0768 **Social Security Number:** 124-89-4567	**Employee ID:** 10024 **Pay Period:** 5/14–5/27

Hours and Earnings

Description	Rate of Pay	Hours / Units	Earnings
Hourly	$22.25	80	$1,780

SECTION 2: WITHHOLDINGS

Description	This Period	YTD
Federal Income Tax	$160.67	$1,606.70
State Income Tax	$41.51	$415.10
Social Security	$110.42	$1,104.20
Medicare	$25.01	$250.10
State Disability	$20.34	$203.40
TOTAL	**$357.95**	**$3,579.50**

SECTION 3: PRE-TAX DEDUCTIONS

Description	This Period	YTD
401K	$100	$1,000

SECTION 4: TOTAL PAY

Description	This Period	YTD
Gross Pay	$1,780	$17,800
Withholdings	$357.95	$3,579.50
Pre-Tax Deductions	$100	$1,000
Net Pay	$1,322.05	$13,220.50

C Where can you find the following information on Leticia's pay stub? Write the section number.

Pay Stub Information	Section
weeks the paycheck covers	1
total amount she takes home	
information about retirement savings	
information about taxes	
hourly wage	

D Work with a partner to answer the questions about Leticia's pay stub. Take turns looking at the pay stub and asking questions.

EXAMPLE: **Student A:** What month is this pay stub from?

                      Student B: May.

1. Did she pay into social security this month? _____

    If so, how much? _____

2. Does she pay Medicare? _____

3. Does she pay state disability insurance? _____

4. How much federal income tax has she paid this year? _____

5. How much money did she make this month before taxes? _____

6. How much state income tax did she pay this month? _____

7. What does she get paid per hour? _____

8. How much has she paid into her 401K this year? _____

E Discuss the questions with a partner.

1. Would you rather get paid every week, twice a month, or once a month? Why?

2. Would you rather get paid a salary or get paid hourly? Why?

F Look at the sentences below. Fill in the information in So's pay stub.

SECTION 1: PERSONAL INFORMATION

Employee Name: So Tran **Check Number:** 0498 **Social Security Number:** _____	**Employee ID:** **Pay Period:** 9/01–9/15

Hours and Earnings

Description	Rate of Pay	Hours / Units	Earnings
Hourly	_____	_____	$960

SECTION 2: WITHHOLDINGS

Description	This Period	YTD
Federal Income Tax	$78.56	_____
State Income Tax	$20.42	$326.72
Social Security	_____	_____
Medicare	_____	$208.80
State Disability	$11.97	$191.52
TOTAL	**$179.19**	**$2,867.04**

SECTION 3: PRE-TAX DEDUCTIONS

Description	This Period	YTD
401K	_____	$800

SECTION 4: TOTAL PAY

Description	This Period	YTD
Gross Pay	_____	$15,360
Withholdings	$179.19	$2,867.04
Pre-Tax Deductions	$50	$800
Net Pay	_____	$12,492.96

1. So paid $55.19 into social security this month. This year, he has paid $883.04.

2. So paid $13.05 into Medicare this month.

3. His social security number is 000-56-8976.

4. He contributes $50 every month into his 401K.

5. He makes $15 an hour.

6. His gross pay was $960.

7. He worked 64 hours this pay period.

8. His year-to-date federal income tax deductions are $1,256.96.

G **CALCULATE** What is So's net pay? (Hint: Subtract his deductions from his gross pay.)

What are the Benefits?

GOAL ▶ Analyze benefit information

A Benefits are extra things that a company offers its employees in addition to a salary. Read the list. Check (✓) the ones given at your current or previous jobs. Add another benefit that you know.

☐ 401K

☐ bonus

☐ dental insurance

☐ disability insurance

☐ maternity leave

☐ health insurance

☐ daycare

☐ family leave

☐ medical leave

☐ overtime

☐ paid personal days

☐ paid sick days

☐ paid vacation days

☐ _____

Life
ONLINE

Companies have policies regarding the use of technology at work. Make sure to become familiar with the policies that affect the use of your personal phone, company computer, etc.

_____

B Listen to the career counselor talk about the benefits that three companies offer. Make notes in the table. 🎧

Company	Health / Dental Insurance	Sick Days	Vacation Days	401K
Set-It-Up Technology	full medical and dental insurance			yes – $1 for every dollar you contribute
Machine Works				
Lino's Ristorante				yes – 50¢ for every dollar you contribute

C **EVALUATE** Which company would you rather work for? Why? Discuss your answer with a partner.

D Read about the benefits offered by some local companies in a small town in Utah.

Employment Monthly
Your source for employment information in Well Springs, Utah

First Marketing offers medical benefits, including dental insurance, disability insurance, family leave, and medical leave to all full-time employees. You'll get paid for up to six sick or personal days you need to take. In addition to the great health benefits, you'll have the opportunity to contribute to a 401K as well as receive bonuses based on productivity at the end of the year. Most employees work full-time and receive time and a half for any overtime they work.

Intepret One is a company that employs hospital interpreters. All full-time employees receive health insurance. You can pay extra for dental insurance, but Interpret One offers medical and family leave. All employees receive a certain number of sick days as well as vacation days, based on how long they have been with the company. They don't offer any bonuses or 401K plans, but they encourage their employees to meet with their financial planner to help plan for retirement.

Ernie's Electrical offers medical, dental, maternity, disability, and family leave to all full- and part-time employees. They give all of their employees three weeks a year to do with as they please—they can be used as sick days, personal days, or vacation days. No employees work overtime at Ernie's Electrical, which helps cut down on costs, but everyone receives a holiday bonus.

E ANALYZE Decide which company or companies would be best for each person.

1. Alicia is a young, hardworking student who can only work part-time. She needs benefits because she lives by herself and has no family in Utah.

_____

2. Rafael needs full benefits and likes to work overtime to make as much money as possible. He already has a 401K from another company that he would like to transfer to his new company.

_____

3. The most important thing for Su is family benefits. She and her husband are ready to start their family, but she still needs to work. She doesn't need dental insurance because her husband's company covers her.

_____

F Complete the statements with a word or phrase from **A**. Then listen to check your answers.

1. ___Disability insurance___ is for those who get injured at work.

2. At times, employees need to take time to care for a sick family member. This is called
   _____.

3. Most companies are required to offer their employees _____ to take care of them and their families when they are sick.

4. Some companies offer a retirement plan called a _____.

5. When a company shares its profits with the employees, each employee gets a
   _____.

6. When a baby comes into the family, the parent is allowed to take _____.

7. When you take a day off to do something for yourself, it is called a _____.

8. Some companies pay _____ when you work more than forty hours a week, or on weekends and holidays.

G **BRAINSTORM** In a group, imagine that you are starting a company. Decide what benefits you will offer. Answer the questions.

1. How many sick days will each employee receive? _____

2. How many personal days will you give each employee? _____

3. How many vacation days will each employee get? _____

4. How much will you pay employees for overtime? _____

5. What other benefits will you offer your employees? List them in your notebook.

Parental leave applies to any parent and is available after both birth and adoption.

Workplace Safety

GOAL ▶ Identify safe workplace behavior

A Look at the pictures. What type of job does each person have? Who needs to consider health issues? Who needs to consider safety issues?

1.

Minh

2.

Francisco

3.

Wassim

4.

Danylo

B Write the name of the person who should wear each health or safety item.

1. a back support belt   _____

2. safety goggles   _____

3. earplugs   _____

4. a hairnet   _____

C Ask your partner if he or she wears safety items at work.

D Read the conversation between Francisco and his manager, Fred. Do you think Fred is right?

Fred: Francisco, why aren't you wearing a back support belt?

Francisco: Oh, I don't need one.

Fred: If you don't wear a belt, you might get hurt.

Francisco: I don't think so. I'm really careful.

Fred: I know, but you could hurt your back if you lift something that is too heavy.

Francisco: You're right. If I get hurt, I might miss work. I could lose a lot of money if I can't work.

Fred: Exactly. Let me get you a belt.

E *Might* and *could* are modals. Underline the modals in the conversation in **D**. Circle the verb that comes after each modal. Then study the chart below.

Modals: *Could* and *Might*			
Subject	**Modal**	**Verb**	**Example Sentence**
I / You / He / She / It / We / They	could	fall	You **could fall**.
	might	miss	I **might miss** work.
The modals *could* and *might* can be used interchangeably because they have a similar meaning when predicting future possibilities. We use them to say that there is a chance that something will happen in the future.			

The man is falling off the ladder. He might get hurt.

F We also use *might* and *could* for potential consequences in conditional sentences with *if* when we are talking about possibilities. Complete the sentences.

1. If Francisco doesn't wear a back support belt, _____ *he could get hurt* _____.

2. If Minh forgets to tie her hair back, _____.

3. José _____ if he doesn't wear a hard hat.

4. Wassim _____ if he doesn't wear safety goggles.

5. Danylo _____ if he doesn't wear earplugs.

6. If Lilly doesn't buckle her seat belt, she _____.

G Look at the safety hazards. What's wrong in each picture?

1.

2.

3.

4.

H **PREDICT** Write sentences in your notebook about what *could* / *might* happen in the situations in **G**.

I Work in a small group to make a list of safety rules for your classroom. Use *could* and *might*.

Good Job!

GOAL ▸ Communicate at work

A **PREDICT** Look at the picture. Is the manager criticizing or complimenting his employee? What do you think they are saying?

Criticize / Compliment

criticize: to say something negative

compliment: to say something nice

B Identify the different types of communication. Write *compliment* or *criticism* next to each sentence.

1. Good job!   *compliment*

2. You need to work a little faster. _____

3. You shouldn't wear that shirt to work. _____

4. That was an excellent presentation. _____

5. You are really friendly to the customers. _____

C **INTERPRET** Are these people responding to criticism or a compliment? Write *compliment* or *criticism* next to each sentence. Then listen and check your answers. 🎧

1. Thanks. I'm glad to hear it. _____

2. I'm sorry. I'll try to do better next time. _____

3. Thanks. _____

4. I'm sorry. I won't wear it again. _____

5. Thank you. I appreciate your telling me that. _____

D Use the sentences and responses in **B** and **C** to make conversations.

EXAMPLE: **Student A:** Good job!

   Student B: Thank you. I appreciate your telling me that.

E Compare the two conversations. Then study the charts.

Employee: Excuse me. Would you mind looking over this report for me before I send it out?

Manager: No, of course not. That's no problem.

Susana: Could you give me a hand with this box?

Coworker: Sure, I'll be right over.

Polite Requests and Responses	
Would you mind helping me?	Polite and formal
Could you help me, **please**?	Polite and friendly
Can you give me a hand?	Polite and informal
Come here!	Very informal and impolite

When we speak to friends or colleagues, it is acceptable to be less formal. When we speak to a boss or a manager, it is polite to be more formal.

Agree	Refuse
Sure.	No. I'm really sorry.
That's fine.	I'm sorry, but I can't.
Of course.	I'd like to, but I can't because . . .
No problem.	
Certainly.	

Rising Intonation for Polite Requests 🎧

Would you mind helping me?

Can you give me a hand?

Tone of Voice for Agreeing and Refusing

When you *agree* to something, your voice should sound *happy* and *upbeat*.

When you *refuse* something, you should sound *apologetic*.

F Listen to these people talk to their bosses, coworkers, and employees. Are they being informal or formal? Check (✓) the correct answer. 🎧

1. ☐ informal ☐ formal   2. ☐ informal ☐ formal

3. ☐ informal ☐ formal   4. ☐ informal ☐ formal

G Complete the workplace conversations with a partner. Then practice your conversations and present them to the class.

Conversation 1

A: That was an excellent project you turned in.

B: _____

A: I'm going to share it with all the other employees.

B: _____

Conversation 2

A: Please don't be late to work anymore.

B: _____

A: It's really affecting your work.

B: _____

Conversation 3

A: _____

B: Sure, I'd be happy to.

A: _____

Conversation 4

A: _____

B: _____

A: _____

B: _____

H Work with a partner. Use the situations to practice making and responding to formal requests, and complimenting and criticizing as necessary.

1. Your manager gave you a good employee review.

2. Ask your coworker to give you a ride home.

3. Your coworker is always late.

4. Ask your boss to help you check some accounts.

Explore the Workforce

GOAL ▶ Discover human resources jobs

A Most companies have a Human Resources (HR) department. What do you think HR does?

RECRUIT

HUMAN
RESOURCES

FIRE

HIRE

INTEGRATE / TRAIN

B **CATEGORIZE** Look at the list below. Some phrases are what a Human Resources department does and other phrases are ways that an HR department supports its employees. Write each in the correct column below.

conducts disciplinary actions	hires the right employees	maintains employee records
offers continuing education	processes payroll	provides career growth
recruits candidates	supports health and wellness	trains and supports managers
updates policies		

What an HR Department Does	How an HR Department Supports Employees

C Go online and find the following information for an HR employee.

Pay: _____

Education Required: _____

Years of Experience Needed: _____

D Look at the map below. What information does it show?

EMPLOYMENT OF HUMAN RESOURCES EMPLOYEES BY STATE

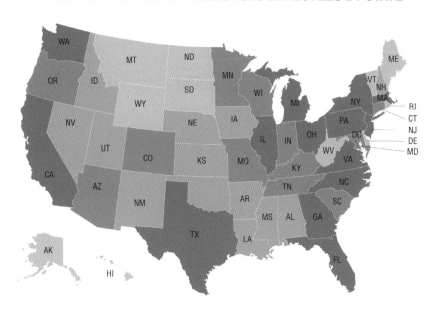

E Answer the following questions with a partner.

1. Which states have the highest number of HR employees?

2. Which states have the fewest?

3. Find your state. How would you describe it? Most HR employees? Fewest HR employees? Or in the middle?

F The following states have the most Human Resources Managers. If California has the most and Florida has the least, can you put the employment numbers in the chart below?

| 10,440 | 12,210 | 24,920 | 7,820 | 11,930 |

According to the chart, you will make the most money as an HR manager if you live in…

a. California   b. Texas   c. New York   d. Illinois

State	Employment	Hourly Mean Wage	Annual Mean Wage
California		$ 74.25	$ 154,430
Illinois		$ 61.93	$ 128,820
Texas		$ 63.60	$ 132,290
New York		$ 86.72	$ 180,380
Florida		$ 56.98	$ 118,520

G **INTERPRET** Read the job ad. Underline phrases you don't understand and discuss with your teacher.

HR Coordinator – Claremont Airport

Claremont, NH $21 an hour (full-time)

The HR Coordinator provides assistance with and facilitates HR support tasks and activities. The position assists with recruiting, administering, hiring and on-boarding, preparing, and maintaining employment records. This position also maintains other human resources documentation, distributes human resources communications as appropriate, and performs all other responsibilities as directed by the business, or as assigned by Management.

Benefits Include:

- Medical, dental and vision
- Vacation and sick time
- 401K retirement savings plan
- Employee meal discounts
- Detailed training and opportunities for professional growth / advancement
- Discounted parking
- Clean, safe, friendly work atmosphere

Minimum Qualifications, Knowledge, Skills, and Work Environment

- Requires high school diploma or General Education Development (GED) diploma
- Requires knowledge of word processing, spreadsheet and data base software
- Demonstrates the ability to interact with the public and coworkers in a friendly, enthusiastic and outgoing manner
- Requires the ability read and comprehend instructions, short correspondence and policy documents, as well as converse comfortably with customers
- Requires basic keyboarding or other repetitive motions

APPLY HERE

H Based on the ad in G, decide if each statement is *True* or *False*. If it's false, make it true.

Example: This job is ~~part~~-time. *False*
(full)

1. You must have a high school diploma or GED to do this job. _____

2. This job offers dental insurance. _____

3. You don't have to know how to use a computer. _____

4. This job is located in New Jersey. _____

5. If you work 40 hours a week, you would make about $2,480 per month. _____

6. This company offers a retirement savings plan. _____

I **REFLECT** Would you be good for this job? Why or why not? Write a paragraph with your ideas on a separate piece of paper.

Review

A Work with a partner. Imagine that you need to hire several new employees for your business. Use the vocabulary from the box to talk about the qualities you are looking for.

ambitious	demanding	funny	interesting	quiet	serious
courteous	friendly	hardworking	patient	respectful	strict

EXAMPLE: **Student A:** I think an ideal employee should be serious.

Student B: I agree. Good employees shouldn't be lazy.

B Circle the correct word in each sentence.

1. Have you seen (my / mine) new pen?

2. (They / Their) cafeteria has delicious food, but (our / ours) is awful.

3. Can I use (your / yours) stapler? I can't find (my / mine.)

4. (Our / Ours) salary is low, but we get lots of tips.

5. (My / Mine) benefits are really good, but (her / hers) are better.

C Match the description to the benefit.

_____ 1. 401K   a. protection against work injuries

_____ 2. bonus   b. a day off to do something for yourself

_____ 3. disability insurance   c. time off to take care of a baby

_____ 4. family leave   d. retirement savings

_____ 5. maternity leave   e. a day off if you are sick

_____ 6. personal day   f. payment when a company shares its profits

_____ 7. sick day   g. time off to care for a sick family member

Learner Log	I can compare employee behavior and attitudes. ☐ Yes ☐ No ☐ Maybe	I can analyze benefit information. ☐ Yes ☐ No ☐ Maybe

D Skim Ali's pay stub and answer the questions below.

SECTION 1: PERSONAL INFORMATION

Employee Name: Ali Ramsey	**Marital Status:** Single
Check Number: 89765	**Pay Period:**
SS Number: 236-49-2524	8/01–8/15

Hours and Earnings

Description	Rate of Pay	Hours / Units	Earnings
Hourly/Day/Monthly	$15.25	56	$854

SECTION 2: WITHHOLDINGS

Description	This Period	YTD
Federal Income Tax	$80.42	$1,206.30
State Income Tax	$21.02	$315.30
Social Security	$65.25	$978.75
Medicare	$12.15	$182.25
State Disability	$10.12	$151.80
TOTAL	**$188.86**	**$2,834.40**

SECTION 3: PRE-TAX DEDUCTIONS

Description	This Period	YTD
401K	$100	$1,500

SECTION 4: TOTAL PAY

Description	This Period	YTD
Gross Pay	$854	$12,810
Withholdings	$188.86	$2,832.90
Pre-Tax Deductions	$100	$1,500
Net Pay	$565.14	$8,377.10

1. Did Ali pay into social security this month? How much? _____

2. Does Ali pay Medicare? _____

3. Does he pay state disability insurance? _____

4. How many hours did he work during this two-week pay period? _____

5. How much federal income tax has Ali paid this year? _____

6. Does he contribute any money to a retirement account? How much? _____

7. How much money did he make this month after taxes? _____

8. How much money did he make this month before taxes? _____

9. How much state income tax did he pay this month? _____

Review

E Complete the following conditional sentences about work situations with *might* or *could*.

1. If you don't mop the wet floor, _____.

2. If the truck driver drives too fast, _____.

3. If those construction workers don't wear earplugs, _____.

4. If the gardener doesn't wear gloves, _____.

F Work with a partner to match the exchanges. Practice them with a partner.

_____ 1. Your report was excellent!   a. I'm so sorry. I've been having car troubles.

_____ 2. I noticed you were late again today. b. It was really interesting to work on, so I couldn't stop!

_____ 3. Can you work a little faster?   c. Thank you. I worked really hard on it.

_____ 4. You finished that project so quickly! d. Yes, I can.

G Work with a partner. Practice making and responding to formal requests using the situations below.

1. Ask your coworker to let you use her computer.

2. Ask your employee to send a fax.

3. Ask your coworker to help you lift a heavy box.

H Use your dictionary to look up different word forms of vocabulary in this unit. Use the new word form in a sentence.

1. nouns: employee, employer   verb: _to employ_

   Our company wants to employ people with good computer skills.

2. noun: promotion   verb: _____

   _____

3. verb: to retire   noun: _____

   _____

Learner Log	I can identify safe workplace behavior. ☐ Yes ☐ No ☐ Maybe	I can communicate at work. ☐ Yes ☐ No ☐ Maybe

192   UNIT 7

Create an Employee Handbook

SOFT SKILL ▶ Collaboration

With your team, you will create one section of an employee handbook. With your class, you will create a complete employee handbook.

1. Form a team with four or five students. Choose a position for each member of your team.

Position	Job Description	Student Name
Student 1: Leader	Check that everyone speaks English and participates.	
Student 2: Secretary	Write information for the handbook with help from the team.	
Student 3: Designer	Design the brochure layout and add artwork with help from the team.	
Students 4/5: Member(s)	Help the secretary and designer with their work.	

2. With your class, look at the list below. Decide which part of the handbook each team will create.

   - Payroll Information
   - Benefits
   - Workplace Safety
   - Workplace Communication

3. Create the text for your section of the employee handbook.

4. Work as a group with your designer to decide what sort of artwork will complement your text.

5. As a class, create a table of contents and a cover. Put your handbook together.

6. Display your handbook so that other classes can see it.

COLLABORATION:
Polite suggestions

As you collaborate, practice making polite suggestions:

I think it would be a great idea if we include….

Why don't we add…?

I think it would be better if….

Reading Challenge

A **Discuss the following questions with a small group.**

1. Have you ever had an experience at your workplace where you felt unsafe? What did you do about it?

2. What types of situations can be unsafe in a workplace? Think of some examples.

3. If you feel unsafe at your workplace, who should you talk to? Do you feel comfortable talking to this person? Why or why not?

B **Read the text. Make a list of vocabulary you don't understand. Find the meanings by discussing with your classmates or looking them up online.**

Vocabulary Word / Phrase	Meaning

C **INFER Choose the best answer.**

1. According to the reading what is NOT a right protected under OSHA?
   a. request an inspection and speak to the inspector
   b. have toxic chemicals removed from your workplace
   c. receive training in a language you understand
   d. get copies of your medical records

2. In line 19, what does the word <u>whistleblower</u> mean?
   a. an employee who complains about unsafe working conditions
   b. an employee who gets fired
   c. an employee who gets transferred to another company
   d. the newest employee at the company

D **Look at the photo and read the caption. What is the the audience watching the demonstration interested in? Why is learning about work safety important?**

E **Choose one of the prompts below and write a paragraph on a separate piece of paper.**

1. How are employee rights different in the United States than in your country?

2. What did you learn from the reading that you didn't know before?

Know Your Rights

The United States Department of Labor has a division whose job it is to protect workers. This division is called the Occupational Safety and Health Administration (OSHA). According to the law, workers are entitled to a safe workplace. It is your employer's duty to make sure that your workplace is free from health and safety hazards. If your employer is not keeping your
5 workplace safe, you have a right to speak up. According to OSHA, you have the right to:

- receive workplace safety and health training in a language that you understand
- work on machines that are safe
- receive required safety equipment, such as gloves or a harness and lifeline for falls
- be protected from toxic chemicals
10 - request an OSHA inspection, and speak to the inspector
- report an injury or illness, and get copies of your medical records
- review records of work-related injuries and illnesses
- see results of tests taken to find workplace hazards

If you think your working conditions are unsafe, you should tell your employer about
15 your concerns. If you are uncomfortable talking to your employer, you can file a confidential complaint with OSHA and request an inspection.

It is against the law for an employee to be fired, demoted, or transferred for complaining to OSHA about unsafe working conditions, since it is a legal right to be able to file a complaint. If this happens, the employee can file a whistleblower complaint. This complaint can be filed with
20 OSHA within 30 days of the unlawful action.

Source: www.osha.gov/workers

Elka Gibbons, a carpenter, demonstrates safe work behavior for the audience. They are learning about building trades at Building Pathways, an organization that creates opportunities for low-income area residents interested in the construction industry.

8 Citizens and Community

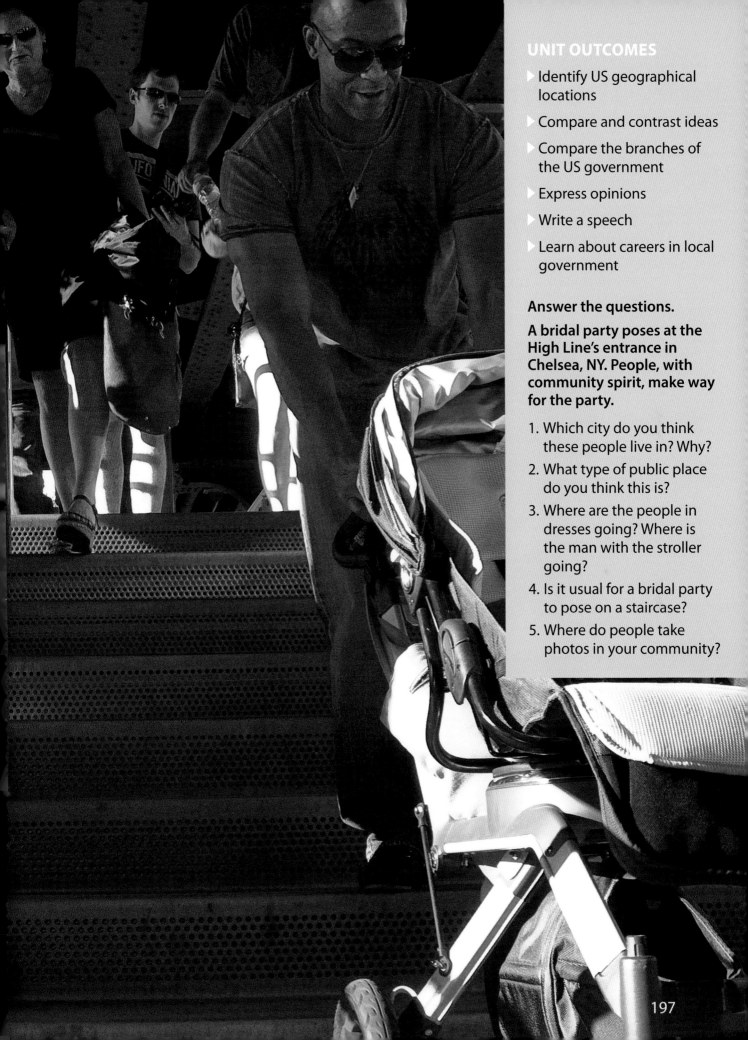

UNIT OUTCOMES

▶ Identify US geographical locations

▶ Compare and contrast ideas

▶ Compare the branches of the US government

▶ Express opinions

▶ Write a speech

▶ Learn about careers in local government

Answer the questions.

A bridal party poses at the High Line's entrance in Chelsea, NY. People, with community spirit, make way for the party.

1. Which city do you think these people live in? Why?

2. What type of public place do you think this is?

3. Where are the people in dresses going? Where is the man with the stroller going?

4. Is it usual for a bridal party to pose on a staircase?

5. Where do people take photos in your community?

The United States

GOAL ▶ Identify US geographical locations

A LOCATE Look at the map of the United States. Write the names of the cities in the spaces provided.

| Philadelphia | Los Angeles | Jamestown | New York | San Francisco | Houston |

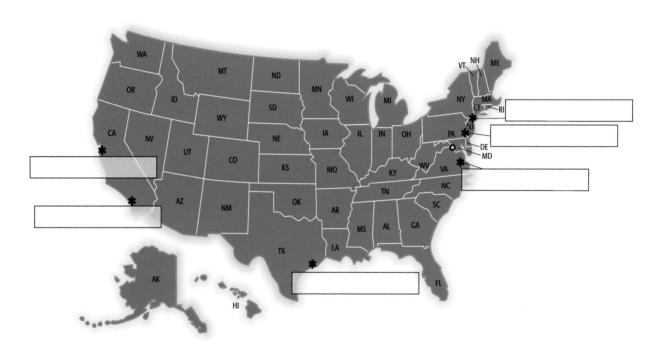

B Look at the map again. Write the names of any other cities you know in the United States.

_____

_____

_____

_____

_____

_____

_____

_____

C Read each state abbreviation and write the full state name. Ask a classmate or your teacher if you need help.

AL	Alabama	MT	_____
AK	_____	NE	Nebraska
AZ	_____	NV	_____
AR	Arkansas	NH	New Hampshire
CA	_____	NJ	_____
CO	_____	NM	_____
CT	Connecticut	NY	_____
DE	Delaware	NC	North Carolina
FL	_____	ND	North Dakota
GA	_____	OH	_____
HI	_____	OK	Oklahoma
ID	_____	OR	_____
IL	Illinois	PA	_____
IN	Indiana	RI	Rhode Island
IA	_____	SC	_____
KS	_____	SD	_____
KY	Kentucky	TN	Tennessee
LA	_____	TX	_____
ME	_____	UT	_____
MD	Maryland	VT	_____
MA	_____	VA	Virginia
MI	Michigan	WA	Washington
MN	_____	WV	_____
MS	Mississippi	WI	_____
MO	Missouri	WY	Wyoming

Note

Washington, DC is not a state.

D **DETERMINE** Ask your partner about the states he or she has visited. Who has visited the most states?

E Look at the pictures of popular tourist attractions in the United States. What are they? Where are they located?

1.

2.

3.

_____

_____

_____

F Listen to the lecture on notable cities in the United States. Match the city with the correct information. Review the vocabulary before you start. 🎧

___*g*___ 1. where the federal government is located

_____ 2. home of the Statue of Liberty

_____ 3. a major port for the Pacific Ocean

_____ 4. a former English colony named after an English king

_____ 5. where the Declaration of Independence was written

_____ 6. the film capital of the world

_____ 7. a major oil producer

_____ 8. where Disney World is located

a. Houston, TX

b. Jamestown, VA

c. Los Angeles, CA

d. New York, NY

e. Philadelphia, PA

f. San Francisco, CA

g. Washington, DC

h. Orlando, FL

G What else do you know about the cities listed in **F**? Discuss your ideas with your classmates and teacher.

H Look at your list of cities in **B**. What are they famous for? Include your own city or the city nearest you.

_____

_____

_____

_____

_____

What's Your Opinion?

GOAL ▶ Compare and contrast ideas

A The mayor is the leader of local government in most cities and towns in the United States. Who is your mayor?

B Imagine that you are getting ready to vote for the new mayor of your city. Read the different points of view of the two candidates below.

Kim Vo Wants to . . .	Dawson Brooks Wants to . . .
• build more parks. • lower class sizes in elementary schools. • lower the tuition at city colleges for immigrant students. • spend tax dollars on wider sidewalks in neighborhoods. • invest money in public transportation. • offer job training programs for homeless people.	• build more highways. • increase the number of teachers per classroom. • raise the tuition at city colleges for immigrant students. • spend tax dollars to improve library facilities. • build more parking structures. • offer incentives for individuals to start their own businesses.

C With a partner, compare the two candidates using *but* and *however*.

EXAMPLE: **Student A:**   Kim Vo wants to build more parks, **but** Dawson Brooks wants to build more highways.

Student B: Dawson Brooks wants to build more highways; **however**, Kim Vo wants to build more parks.

D **COMPARE** Write two sentences comparing Kim Vo and Dawson Brooks using *but* or *however*.

1. _____

_____

2. _____

_____

E **EXPLAIN** Which issues in **B** are most important to you? Why? Write a paragraph on a separate piece of paper.

F Ask your classmates about their feelings on the topics below. Think of your own topic for the last question.

Name	Topic	Agree	Disagree
	increasing the number of students in our class		

Name	Topic	Agree	Disagree
	building more schools in our community		

Name	Topic	Agree	Disagree
	adding more bike lanes		

Name	Topic	Agree	Disagree

G Study the chart with your classmates and teacher.

Comparing and Contrasting Ideas	
If two people share the same opinion, use *both … and* or *neither … nor*.	
Both Enrico **and** Liz **Neither** Enrico **nor** Liz	**want** to increase the number of students in our class. **wants** to increase the number of students in our class.
If two people don't share the same opinion, use *but* or *however*.	
Enrico agrees with adding more bike lanes,	**but** Liz doesn't.
Ali doesn't agree with adding more bike lanes;	**however**, Suzana does.
Punctuation note: Use a semicolon (;) before and a comma (,) after *however*.	

H **Complete each sentence with** *both, and, neither, nor, but,* **or** *however.*

1. Neither Alicia _____ Hoa wants the city to build a school instead of a park.

2. _____ Kim and Su want to increase the number of hours that our class meets.

3. Jeeva thinks the library should be open seven days a week; _____, Adam thinks five days a week is plenty.

4. Bruno believes all children should study a second language, _____ Liza thinks children should learn only their native language.

5. _____ Lim nor Jeremy wants more homework.

6. Both Elizabeth _____ Parker want to do more writing in class.

I **COMPARE** **Look back at the information you collected from your classmates in F. Write sentences comparing their ideas.**

1. _____

_____

_____

2. _____

_____

_____

3. _____

_____

_____

4. _____

_____

_____

LESSON 3 | US Government

GOAL ▶ Compare the branches of the US government

A Look at the three branches that make up the US government. What do you know about them?

1.

Executive

2.

Legislative

3.

Judicial

B Read about the US government. Then answer the questions after each section.

The US Government

The US government has three branches—the executive branch, the legislative branch, and the judicial branch. The government was set up this way so no one person would have too much power. With three branches, each branch balances out the others.

The Executive Branch

In the executive branch are the president, the vice president, and the cabinet. The president is the leader of the country and of the executive branch. He or she can sign new laws, prepare the budget, and command the military. The vice president helps the president and is the leader of the Senate. Both the president and the vice president serve for four years and can be reelected only once. The president's cabinet is a group of experts who advise the president. The president chooses his cabinet members. They include the Secretary of State, the Secretary of Defense, and the Secretary of Education.

1. What does the president do? _____

2. What does the vice president do? _____

3. How long do the president and vice president serve? _____

4. What does the cabinet do? _____

5. Do voters elect cabinet members? _____

The Legislative Branch

The legislative branch, also known as Congress, makes the laws for the United States. Congress has the power to declare war, collect taxes, borrow money, control immigration, set up a judicial and postal system, and the most important power, to make laws.

This branch has the greatest connection to the people of the United States because this branch represents citizens. Congress has two parts—the House of Representatives and the Senate. The House of Representatives has 435 state representatives. Each state gets a certain number of representatives, based on its population. Each representative serves for two years and can be reelected. The Senate has 100 senators, two from each of the 50 states. Senators serve for six years and can also be reelected.

1. What is another name for the legislative branch? _____

2. What is the most important thing this branch does? _____

3. What are the two parts of this branch called? _____

4. How many representatives are in the House? _____

5. What determines the number of representatives each state gets? _____

6. How long do representatives serve? _____

7. How many senators does each state have? _____

8. How long do senators serve? _____

The Judicial Branch

The third branch of the US government is the judicial branch, which includes the Supreme Court and the federal courts. The job of the courts is to interpret the laws made by the legislative branch. The Supreme Court is the highest court in the United States and has nine judges called *justices*. The justices listen to cases and make judgments based on the Constitution and the laws of the United States. The president and Congress choose the justices of the Supreme Court.

1. What is the role of the judicial branch? _____

2. What is the highest court in the United States? _____

3. How does a person become a judge on the Supreme Court? _____

_____

C Most cities have government officials who are elected to help run the city. Listen to the following people talk about their jobs and fill in the table with their duties. 🎧

Official	Duties
tax assessor	1. helps county set tax rates 2. decides on the value of property
city clerk	1. _____ 2. _____
city council member	1. _____ 2. _____
superintendent of schools	1. _____ 2. _____
mayor	1. _____ 2. _____

D **EVALUATE** Discuss the positions in the table above with a group. Which position would you most like to have? Why? Which one would you least like to have? Why? Write a paragraph answering these questions.

_____

_____

_____

_____

_____

_____

_____

_____

_____

_____

Community Concerns

GOAL ▶ Express opinions

A Cherie lives in a small town in California that is not as nice as it used to be. Read about the problems in Cherie's community. 🎧

A crossing guard helps children cross the street at the entrance to the Rossmoor neighborhood.

My name is Cherie. I live in a small community called Rossmoor in California. I moved here about ten years ago with my family because we wanted to live in a nice, safe community, but many things have happened in the past ten years.

First of all, the neighborhood schools are overcrowded. Because our school system is so good, many families from outside neighborhoods send their kids to our schools. There are over 35 students in each classroom.

Another problem is that there are some people with mental health issues on our streets. It sometimes makes me nervous to have my kids walking home by themselves. I wish they could take a bus, but that's another problem. We don't have any public transportation here. When Rossmoor was first built, many wealthy people moved here. They all had cars, so there was no need for public transportation, but now things have changed. I think it's time for me to go to a city council meeting to see what I can do for our community.

B Cherie talks about three different problems. List them below.

1. _____

2. _____

3. _____

C BRAINSTORM With a group, discuss possible solutions to each problem in Cherie's community. Write your ideas below. Report your answers to the class.

Problem	Possible Solutions
overcrowded schools	1. 2.
people with mental health issues	1. 2.
no public transportation	1. 2.

D Rossmoor is a nice place to live, but like every community, it has some problems. Match each problem with a possible solution. Then compare answers with a partner and say if you agree or disagree with each solution.

_____ 1. Visitors park in resident parking spaces.

_____ 2. People don't clean up after their pets.

_____ 3. Teenagers are out late at night getting into trouble.

_____ 4. The parks are not maintained.

a. Set a curfew for teenagers.

b. Fine people who don't clean up after their pets.

c. Give tickets to visitors who park in resident spaces.

d. Raise taxes to help with recreation improvements.

E We use *should* to give a strong suggestion. Study the chart below with your teacher.

Modal *Should*			
Subject	*Should*	Base Verb	
The city council	**should**	set	a curfew for teenagers.
People	**should**	clean up	after their pets.

F With your group, use *should* to talk about the solutions you wrote in C.

G **FORMULATE** In a group, form a city council. Decide how you will solve the following problems and present your ideas to the class. The class will vote on which group would be the best city council.

1. Our city has cut lanes of traffic to put bike lanes in. This is dangerous for the bikers and has caused a lot of traffic in our city. How can we fix this?

2. The house prices are going up in our community. It's difficult to find affordable rent and almost impossible to buy a house. Many people are moving away from the community to find cheaper housing. The community wants to maintain diversity, but only the very wealthy can afford to stay. What should we do about the housing costs?

3. The town's river was very dirty, but groups of citizens did a lot to clean it up. We want to increase taxes so we can build a new park along the river, but the growing town needs a new hospital and more office space too. Is there a way to make everyone happy?

Life ONLINE Did you know many cities and towns have an app that residents can use to access local services? You can check parking access, report a broken traffic signal or street light, alert the authorities about a fallen tree or wire, or even request a trash cleanup, right from your phone. You do not need to be a citizen, pay a fee, or submit your personal information to use municipal apps to take advantage of local services. Look in your app store to see if your community has an app like this.

Bike lanes make commuting safer for cyclists in big cities like New York.

If I Were President

GOAL ▶ Write a speech

A Rosario's teacher asked her to write a paragraph about what she would do if she became president of the United States. Read what she wrote below.

> *If I were president, nobody would be poor or homeless. Personally, I think if people had more money, they wouldn't commit crimes. In my opinion, we shouldn't spend so much money on the military. If scientists didn't have to build weapons, they would have more time to study other things. Maybe they would find a cure for cancer. I think that I'd be a great president!*

B Study these expressions with your classmates and teacher. Underline the ones Rosario used in her paragraph above.

In my opinion, …	I believe that …
As I see it, …	I think that …
Personally, I think …	I feel that …

C PLAN On a separate piece of paper, write your opinion about the topics. Use the expressions from B.

1. the environment _I think we should be more concerned about the environment._

2. crime _____

3. homework _____

4. public transportation in my city _____

5. free English classes _____

D Study the chart with your classmates and teacher.

		Contrary-to-Fact Conditional Statements			
If	**Subject**	**Past Tense Verb + Noun**	**Subject**	**Modal**	**Base Verb + Noun**
If	I	had more money,	I	would	buy a house.
If	you	didn't have the flu,	you	would	go to work.
If	he	had more time,	he	would	take more classes.
If	she	were rich,	she	could	help her parents.
If	we	gave food to charities,	we	could	help our community.
If	they	weren't so tired,	they	could	come to the movies.

Contrary-to-fact (or unreal) conditional statements are sentences that are not true and that the speaker thinks will probably never be true.
Note: In written English, we use *were* instead of *was* in contrary-to-fact statements, but in spoken English, we often use *was* with the following subjects: I, he, and she.

E Complete the sentences below with the correct form of the verb in parentheses.

1. I _____would give_____ (give) money to the homeless if _____I were_____ (be) president.

2. If people _____ (have) more money, they _____ (be) happier.

3. If the president _____ (spend) more on health, scientists _____ (discover) a cure for cancer.

4. If our classes _____ (be) larger, the teacher _____ (not have) much time for each student.

5. Maria _____ (go) to medical school if she _____ (be) younger.

F Look at the list of city officials on page 206. Write a contrary-to-fact conditional statement for each official. Then share your statements with a partner.

EXAMPLE: If I were the tax assessor, I would lower taxes.

_____

_____

_____

_____

_____

G **What would you do if you were president? Talk about the things you would like to change.**

Student A: What would you do if you were president?

Student B: Let's see. I think we need to improve our schools.

Student A: How would you do that?

Student B: I would pay teachers more. I would spend money on things like computers.

H **Think about the following topics. What would you do if you were president? Write your ideas.**

Topic	My Ideas
eliminating the death penalty	
raising the retirement age to 70	
raising the cost of gasoline so people would drive less	
smoking in public places	
raising the minimum wage	
building casinos to raise money for schools	

I **VISUALIZE** Using the ideas you wrote above, write a paragraph about what you would do if you were president. Use Rosario's paragraph in **A** as an example. Then share your paragraph with the class. Who would the class elect to be president?

_____

_____

_____

_____

_____

_____

LESSON 6

Explore the Workforce

GOAL ▶ Learn about careers in local government

A What jobs do you think of when you hear the phrase *local government*? Write them below.

_____

B **BRAINSTORM** There are many different kinds of local government jobs. Look at each of the categories below and brainstorm at least two jobs for each.

Category	Jobs
Police protection	
Health	
Elementary and secondary education	
Public welfare	
Parks and recreation	
Judicial and legal	
Transit	

C **REFLECT** Answer the questions below. Then share your answers with a partner.

1. Which job category was the easiest to come up with jobs for?

2. Which category was the most difficult to come up with jobs for?

3. What other local government categories are missing from the chart in **B**? Add three more to the chart and come up with jobs.

PUBLIC EMPLOYMENT: TOP 13 STATE AND LOCAL JOB CATEGORIES

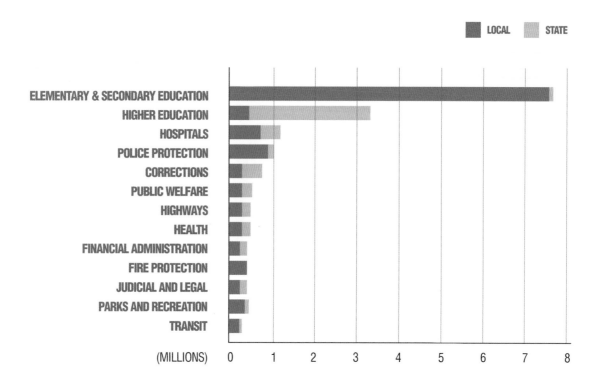

1. If you want to get a local government job, in which category do you think you will have the best chance? _____. Why do you think this is true? _____

_____

2. If you want to get a local government job, in which category do you think you will have the second-best chance? _____

3. What type of job in local government will be most difficult to find? _____.
Why do you think this is true? _____

4. List three categories that you would like to consider getting.

_____

5. What are two categories that you would never want to get a job in?

_____

E Take a poll in your class. Find out what job each person has. (*Student* and *stay-at-home parent* are acceptable answers). Then complete the table below. You will have to come up with your own categories based on the answers you get. (Ask your teacher for help.)

Category	Jobs

F Using the information from **E**. Create a bar graph similar to the one in **D**.

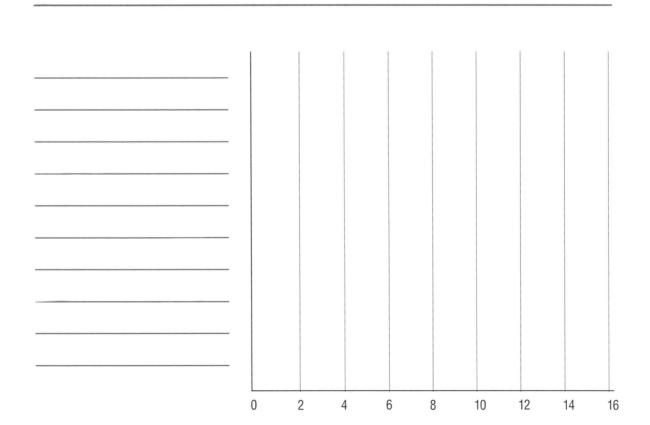

Review

A Write the full name of each state next to its abbreviation. See how many you can remember before you look back at page 199.

1. NY _____ 2. CA _____

3. WA _____ 4. FL _____

5. TX _____ 6. ME _____

7. IL _____ 8. NV _____

9. HI _____ 10. NJ _____

B Read the table below. Write sentences using *both . . . and, neither . . . nor, but,* and *however.*

EXAMPLE: _Both Sophia and Jamal want to increase class size._ _____

Name	Topic	Agree	Disagree
Sophia	increasing the number of students in our class	✓	
Jamal		✓	
Sophia	building more parks in the community		✓
Jamal		✓	
Sophia	providing more recycling centers	✓	
Jamal			✓
Sophia	building more freeways		✓
Jamal			✓

1. _____

_____

2. _____

_____

3. _____

_____

Learner Log	I can identify US geographical locations. ☐ Yes ☐ No ☐ Maybe	I can compare and contrast ideas. ☐ Yes ☐ No ☐ Maybe

C Check (✓) the correct branch of government for each statement.

	Legislative	Executive	Judicial
1. listens to cases and makes judgments			
2. interprets the laws			
3. signs new laws			
4. includes the president's cabinet			
5. includes the House of Representatives			
6. makes laws			
7. can control immigration			
8. commands the military			
9. includes the Congress			
10. chooses the justices of the Supreme Court			

D Look at the community problems below. Write a solution for each problem using *should*.

1. **Problem:** traffic on the freeways

   Solution: _The city should build more carpool lanes._

2. **Problem:** smoking in parks near playgrounds

   Solution: _____

3. **Problem:** cars driving too fast in residential areas

   Solution: _____

4. **Problem:** potholes

   Solution: _____

5. **Problem:** high crime

   Solution: _____

Learner Log	I can compare the branches of the US government.	I can express opinions.
	☐ Yes ☐ No ☐ Maybe	☐ Yes ☐ No ☐ Maybe

Review

E Complete these contrary-to-fact conditionals with the correct form of the verbs in parentheses.

1. I _____ (work) faster if I _____ (have) a computer.

2. If she _____ (learn) an accounting program, she _____ (apply) for a new job.

3. If it _____ (stop) raining, we _____ (play) outside.

4. If the town _____ (buy) more land, we _____ (build) schools.

F What would you do if you were mayor of your city? Write a paragraph stating your opinions about various local issues. Then say what you would do if you were mayor.

In my opinion, the public transportation system in this town is very poor. The buses are always

late because there is too much traffic. If I were mayor, I would build a subway system and . . .

_____

_____

_____

_____

_____

G Practice writing an entry in a vocabulary book. Add any new words you have learned inside or outside of class.

EXAMPLE: **Word:** legislature

Part of speech: noun

Definition: a branch of the US government that passes laws

Related word(s): legislation *(n)*, legislate *(v)*

Example sentence: The <u>legislature</u> passed a new law on gasoline taxes.

Learner Log	I can write a speech. ☐ Yes ☐ No ☐ Maybe

Run for Mayor
SOFT SKILL ▶ Presentation

With your team, you will run a mayoral campaign. You will write a list of community problems and your solutions, and create a flyer that will help you gain votes. You will also write the speech that you would give if you were elected mayor.

1. Form a team with four or five students. Choose a position for each member of your team.

Position	Job Description	Student Name
Student 1: Leader	Check that everyone speaks English. Check that everyone participates.	
Student 2: Secretary	Write down the community problems, possible solutions, and the speech with help from the team.	
Student 3: Designer	Create the flyer.	
Students 4/5: Members	Help the secretary and the designer with their work.	

2. Imagine someone on your team is running for mayor of your city. Answer the following questions:

   Why does your candidate want to be mayor?

   Why would he or she be the best mayor?

3. Come up with a list of community problems and your solutions to those problems.

4. Create a flyer including all your information and any appropriate pictures or art.

5. Write the speech that you would give as mayor.

6. Present your flyer and speech to the class.

PRESENTATION:
Public Speaking

Practice your presentation before you present to the class. It would be great if you could memorize your speech, but if you can't:

- Read it over many times so you don't have to keep your eyes glued on your paper.
- Look up from your paper often and make eye contact with your audience.
- Speak clearly and slowly so you can be understood.

Reading Challenge

A Look at the photo. What do you see? Where is the city located? Is it large or small? Discuss your ideas.

B Look at a map of the United States. Find the state of New Mexico. What do you know about this state? Have you ever been there? Discuss with a small group.

C Read the text. There are four quotes in the readings. Underline them as you read.

D **CHOOSE** Which quote do you like the best? Write it below.

_____

_____

_____

E **SCAN** What do the words mean? Scan the reading and match.

_____ 1. municipal   a. the method used to solve a problem

_____ 2. cliché   b. by or among ordinary people

_____ 3. approach   c. showing sympathy for someone

_____ 4. compassionate   d. relating to a town, city, or local government

_____ 5. grassroots   e. the act of being mentally stimulated to do or feel something

_____ 6. inspiration   f. a common thought that is used too often to be meaningful

F **ANALYZE** Look at the quote you chose in **D**. What does it mean? Using at least two new vocabulary words from **E**, write a paragraph.

_____

_____

_____

_____

_____

_____

_____

_____

A view from Picacho Peak of the supermoon over Las Cruces, NM

Time for a Change 🎧

In January of 2022, the city of Las Cruces, New Mexico did something it had never done before. The citizens voted for and elected an all-female city council. Nationwide, about thirty percent of municipal offices (including mayoral offices, city councils and other similar government positions) are held by women. So, when Las Cruces, a city a of about
5 100,000 people in the southern part of New Mexico, elected their new city council, it was clear that the residents wanted a change.

Becki Graham, one of the newly-elected city councilors said, "I think that I'm coming into it with this idea that, as cliché as it may sound, maybe this is going to be a space where leaders are more willing to listen to one another."
10 Councilor Johana Bencomo agreed. "I just think that our approach to some of the things that really matter to Las Cruces will be inherently different, and honestly, I think more compassionate." Bencomo hopes than an all-female city council, especially one with women of color, can increase public support for important issues, such as increasing the minimum wage. "I really do feel like it's been a lot of grassroots power-building that has allowed for people who
15 never traditionally saw themselves in leadership positions to take ownership of it and represent their communities," she said.

Jessica Velasquez, who is the chairwoman of the Democratic Party of New Mexico, watched the election results come in the November election with her 12-year-old daughter. "Watching my daughter's face light up when she heard that Las Cruces had elected an all-woman city
20 council for the first time in history … the look of inspiration and happiness on her face said it all for me," she said.

Life ONLINE

City Hall In Your Pocket

Before You Watch

A Check (✓) the city services you use. Then share your answers with a partner.

☐ 1. I use public transportation.

☐ 2. I use the library.

☐ 3. I pay utility bills.

☐ 4. I pay to park on the street.

☐ 5. I go to public parks.

☐ 6. I use public garbage and recycling cans.

B Read the words. Then complete the sentences.

collects	immediate	issue	locate	resident	resolve	restriction	submit

1. If you fix a problem, you _____ the problem.

2. An _____ is a problem or something that needs to be fixed.

3. When you _____ a question or a comment online, you send it to someone.

4. When the city _____ garbage, they take it or pick it up.

5. A _____ is a rule that tells you what you cannot do.

6. A _____ is a person who lives in a certain place.

7. _____ means right away.

8. When you _____ something, you find out where it is.

C You are going to watch a video about municipal 311 apps that can help you find city services. Which services do you think the video will talk about?

While You Watch

D Watch the video. Check (✓) the services that municipal 311 apps offer.

☐ 1. paying for parking

☐ 2. delivering pizza

☐ 3. sending an ambulance

☐ 4. finding libraries

☐ 5. reporting broken traffic lights

☐ 6. finding a lost dog

☐ 7. fixing your car

☐ 8. getting restaurant recommendations

☐ 9. collecting garbage

☐ 10. requesting a taxi

☐ 11. locating police stations

☐ 12. showing maps of parks

After You Watch

E Read each sentence. Choose *T* if it is true and *F* if it is false.

1. Many cities have both a phone number and an app for city services.   **T   F**

2. All cities offer the same services on their apps.   **T   F**

3. 311 apps let you tell city hall about issues in your community.   **T   F**

4. You should call 311 if you see someone in danger.   **T   F**

5. Only US citizens can use 311 apps.   **T   F**

6. 311 apps let residents see how their taxes are used.   **T   F**

F Work with a partner. Write three city services you heard about in the video. Which one is most useful? Are there other services you want to see from your city? Do you plan to use 311 or a municipal services app? Why or why not?"

_____

_____

_____

Life Skills Video Practice

My Schedule Is Crazy

A BEFORE Discuss the questions with a partner.

1. Tell your partner your schedule next week. Who has a busier schedule?

2. Where is your favorite place to study? Why?

B WHILE Watch the video and complete the parts of the conversation.

Naomi: Treat your studies in the same way, and your grades will (1) ___*improve*___.

Hector: That's a great (2) _____, thanks.

Naomi: If you get (3) _____, you'll feel more productive.

Hector: (4) _____ give it a try. What have I got to lose, right?

C AFTER Circle the correct word to complete each sentence.

1. There's too much noise and it's difficult for Hector to (communicate / concentrate).

2. Naomi suggests that Hector should (make time / write down) where and when he's going to study.

3. Naomi tells Hector a schedule will make him (productive / smarter).

UNIT 2 It's Faster – and More Expensive.

A BEFORE Discuss the questions with a partner.

1. What type of computer do you use at home, work, or school?

2. Do you prefer to use a laptop or a desktop computer? Why?

B WHILE Watch the video and complete the parts of the conversation.

Mr. Sanchez: Compare the laptop to a (1) ___*desktop*___ computer.

Mrs. Sanchez: The desktop computer is a lot bigger and heavier than the (2) _____.

Mrs. Sanchez: The laptop is smaller than the desktop, but it's also (3) _____ than the desktop.

Mrs. Sanchez: Which one has the (4) _____ memory?

C AFTER Show the correct order of events by writing a number next to each sentence.

a. _____ Mr. Sanchez says the laptop is on sale.

b. _____ Mr. Sanchez says Hector needs a computer.

c. _____ Hector comes home.

d. _____ The Sanchez's agree to surprise Hector.

e. _____ The Sanchez's compare laptops and desktops.

UNIT 3 How Much Is the Rent?

A BEFORE Discuss the questions with a partner.

1. What do you like about your house or apartment?

2. What don't you like about your house or apartment?

B WHILE Watch the video and complete the parts of the conversation.

Naomi: This is a lot (1) _____bigger_____ than the other apartment.

Landlord: And it's a little (2) _____ expensive too.

Naomi: How much is the (3) _____?

Landlord: It's $1,700 a (4) _____.

Landlord: I don't think you'll find anything (5) _____ around here.

C AFTER Circle the answer to complete each sentence.

1. The landlord is showing them an (apartment / house).

2. The master bedroom is (smaller / bigger) than the other bedrooms.

3. The rent doesn't include (garbage / electricity).

4. There's another apartment (downstairs / upstairs) for less rent.

UNIT 4 I'd Like to Open an Account.

A BEFORE Discuss the questions with a partner.

1. What type of bank account(s) do you know about? What are they for?

2. What do you need to open a bank account? Make a list with your partner.

B WHILE Watch the video and complete the parts of the conversation.

Naomi: By the way, when will the money be (1) _____?

Mr. Sanchez: Since you (2) _____ cash, the money's available now.

Naomi: Later on, can I open a (3) _____ account online?

Mr. Sanchez: You can (4) _____ money from your checking account.

C AFTER Put the sentences in order to make a conversation.

_____ **Customer:** A savings account.

_____ **Clerk:** What kind of account would you like to open?

_____ **Customer:** Hello. I'd like to open an account.

_____ **Clerk:** How much money would you like to deposit?

UNIT 5 Exercise Is Good for You.

A BEFORE Discuss the questions with a partner.

1. How can you stay healthy at work?

2. What are your healthy and unhealthy habits at work or school?

B WHILE Watch the video and complete the parts of the conversation.

Mr. Patel: What's (1) _____ on here?

Mateo: We're (2) _____, Mr. Patel. Why don't you join us?

Mr. Patel: I can't do that. I haven't touched my (3) _____ in years.

Mateo: It's (4) _____ for you. C'mon, try it.

C AFTER Match the parts to complete the sentences.

_____ 1. Mateo   a. are bad for you because they have a lot of calories.

_____ 2. Exercise   b. can create some serious health problems.

_____ 3. Too much sugar   c. has a healthy lifestyle.

_____ 4. Soda and candy   d. will prevent your muscles from getting tight.

UNIT 6 How's Your New Job, Hector?

A BEFORE Discuss the questions with a partner.

1. What information should you put on a resume?

2. What are some good ways to prepare for a job interview?

B WHILE Watch the video and complete the parts of the conversation.

Hector: I just feel I could be (1) _____*doing*_____ something more.

Naomi: Wow, that's really (2) _____.

Hector: Well, I'd have to (3) _____ on my hours at the store. Mr. Patel might not like that.

Mateo: He won't (4) _____ you. He'll love you even more.

Naomi: If that's what you want to do, you (5) _____ go for it.

C AFTER Write *newspaper* or *clothing store* next to the pros.

1. going different places   _____

2. working with Mateo   _____

3. meeting interesting people and getting paid for it   _____

4. getting discounts on nice clothes   _____

5. leading to a career   _____

No Wonder I Need to Save!

A **BEFORE** **Discuss the questions with a partner.**

1. What deductions can you usually see on a paycheck?

2. What job benefits are important to you?

B **WHILE** **Watch the video and complete the parts of the conversation.**

Mateo: You pay about $50 for health (1) _____, right?

Hector: And another $50 goes into my (2) _____.

Mateo: That's good. That's another (3) _____. Anything else?

Hector: Well, there's (4) _____, dental insurance, and transportation.

Mateo: As you can see, almost one-third of your check is (5) _____.

C **AFTER** **Write _T_ for True and _F_ for False.**

1. Mr. Patel gives Hector and Mateo their paychecks every Thursday. _____

2. Hector pays about $50 in health insurance each week. _____

3. Mateo pays $50 into his 401K every week. _____

4. Hector has dental insurance, but Mateo doesn't. _____

5. Mr. Patel gives a bonus at the end of the year. _____

Let's Get Ready to Play

A **BEFORE** **Discuss the questions with a partner.**

1. Which subject do you know more about; History, Geography, or Science? Why?

2. With a partner write as many US states as you can. Do not look in your student book. Compare your list with the rest of the class.

B **WHILE** **Watch the video and complete the conversation.**

Naomi: OK, here's the first question. Which state is in the center of the country:

(1) _____, Colorado, or Kansas?

Hector: I know—um, (2) _____?

Mateo: Colorado and Arizona are both in the Southwest. So it must be (3) _____.

Naomi: Kansas is in the central United States. It's in a region called the (4) _____.

C **AFTER** **Write _T_ for True and _F_ for False.**

1. Mateo's specialty is history. _____

2. New York City is the oldest city in the United States. _____

3. Colorado is in the center of the country. _____

4. Naomi answered the second question correctly. _____

Stand Out Vocabulary List

cause
cavities
cholesterol
cold
conditions
dietitian
digestion
diseases
dizzy
effect
fat
grain
fiber
habit
headache
health-related careers
healthy weight
illness
liver
lungs
maintain
massage therapist
nutrients
nutritionist
occupational therapist
parts of the body (internal and external)
physical fitness
physical therapist
physical therapist assistant / aide
protein
recreational
saturated fat
serving size
sick
sodium
sore
stress
sugar
sunscreen
vitamins

UNIT 6 pp. 144–169

assemble
abbreviations

average salary
career
character traits
communication skills
connection
critical thinking skills
custodian
elderly
employment agency
enthusiasm
general management careers
general manager
hiring
insurance forms
job
job application
job titles
leadership skills
nursing home
organizational skills
operate
personality
position
practice
recruit
resume
self-confidence
sensitivity
sew
skills
starting salary
supplies
technical skills
technician
title
training
warmth

UNIT 7 pp. 170–195

401K
ambitious
back support belt
behavior
bonus

check number
compliment
conduct
continuing education
courteous
coworker
criticism
demanding
dental insurance
disability insurance
earnings
earplugs
easygoing
family leave
federal
fire
gloves
gross pay
hairnet
hard hat
hire
health insurance
Human Resources (HR)
Human Resources Department
ideal
marital status
maternity leave
medical leave
Medicare
net pay
number
overtime
patient
payroll
personal days
pre-tax deductions
processes payroll
rate of pay
request
retirement
safety goggles
safety items
seat belt
sick days

social security (SS)
state
state disability
strict
tax deductions
total amount
updates policies
vacation days
year-to-date
year-to-date (YTD) total

UNIT 8 pp. 196–221

cabinet
capital
casinos
city officials
colony
Congress
curfew
death penalty
elementary and secondary education
executive
fine
House of Representatives
incentives
judicial
legal
legislative
local government
names of states
overcrowded
parks & recreation
port
president
producer
resident
retirement
Senate
Supreme Court
tickets
transit
tuition
vice president
wage
wealthy

Stand Out Grammar Reference

UNIT 1

0%	50%	100%

| never | rarely | sometimes | usually | always |

Placement Rules for Frequency Adverbs	Examples
Before the main verb	Luisa *always / usually / often* **goes** running. She *sometimes / rarely / never* **does** yoga.
After the main verb *be*	She **is** *usually* busy on the weekends.
Sometimes / usually / often can come at the beginning or at the end of a sentence	**Usually / Sometimes** Luisa starts work in the morning. Luisa starts work in the morning **sometimes / often**.
Between the subject and the verb in short answers	Yes, **she** *always* **does**. / No, **she** *usually* **isn't**.
Rarely and *never* are negative words. Do not use *not* and *never* in the same sentence.	Correct: She **never** plays tennis. Incorrect: She ~~doesn't~~ *never* plays tennis.

Future Time Clauses with *When*			
When + Subject	Verb (Present)	Subject + *Will*	Base Verb
When Bolin	graduates,	he will	**apply** for a new position at work.*
When his parents	come to the United States,	he will	**buy** a house.

*Note: Place a comma after the *when* clause when it begins the sentence. The order of the clauses does not matter. You can also say, *Bolin will apply for a new position at work when he graduates.*

UNIT 2

To Get Something Done				
Subject	*Get*	Object	Past Participle	Example Sentence
I	get	my hair	cut.	I **get my hair cut** every month. (present)
She	got	her clothes	cleaned.	She **got her clothes cleaned** yesterday. (past)

Comparatives				
	Adjective	Comparative	Rule	Example Sentence
Short adjectives	cheap	cheaper	Add *-er* to the end of the adjective.	Your computer was **cheaper** than my computer.
Long adjectives	expensive	more expensive	Add *more* before the adjective.	The new computer was **more expensive** than the old one.
Irregular adjectives	good bad	better worse	These adjectives are irregular.	The computer at school is **better** than this one.
Remember to use *than* after a comparative adjective followed by a noun.				

Superlatives

	Adjective	Superlative	Rule	Example Sentence
Short adjectives	cheap	the cheapest	Add -*est* to the end of the adjective.	Your computer is **the cheapest.**
Long adjectives	expensive	the most expensive	Add *most* before the adjective.	He bought **the most expensive** computer in the store.
Irregular adjectives	good bad	the best the worst	These adjectives are irregular.	The computers at school are **the best.**
Always use *the* before a superlative.				

Must vs. *Have to*

Subject	Modal	Base Verb	Example Sentence
I / You / We / They	have to must	save pay off	I **have to** save money for a vacation. I **must** pay off my credit card every month.
He / She / It	has to must	keep	She **has to** keep track of her money. He **must** keep track of his money.

UNIT 3

Comparatives Using Nouns

Use *more* or *fewer* to compare count nouns.	Our new apartment has **more bedrooms** than our old one. Our old apartment had **fewer bedrooms** than our new one.
Use *more* or *less* to compare noncount nouns.	Rachel's apartment gets **more light** than Pablo's apartment. Pablo's apartment gets **less light** than Rachel's apartment.

Superlatives Using Nouns

Use *the most* or *the fewest* for count nouns.	Rachel's apartment has **the most bedrooms.** Phuong's apartment has **the fewest bedrooms.**
Use *the most* or *the least* for non-count nouns.	Rachel's apartment has **the most light.** Phuong's apartment has **the least light.**

Review: *Yes / No* Questions and Answers with *Do*

Questions				
Do	Subject	Base Verb	Example Question	Short Answers
Do	I / You / We / They	have	Do they have a yard?	Yes, they do. / No, they don't.
Does	he / she / it	want	Does she want air-conditioning?	Yes, she does. / No, she doesn't.

Information Questions

Question Words	Example Questions
How	**How** may I help you?
What	**What** is your current address?
When	**When** would you like your service turned off?

Past Continuous

Subject	*Be*	Verb + *ing*	Example Sentence
I / He / She / It	was	making	I **was making** breakfast.
You / We / They	were	studying	They **were studying.**

Use the past continuous to talk about things that started in the past and continued for a period of time.

Past Continuous Using *While*

Subject	*Be*	Verb + *ing*	Example Sentence
I / He / She / It	was	making	While I **was making** dinner, I saw a mouse.
You / We / They	were	studying	The electricity went out while we **were studying.**

To connect two events that happened in the past, use the past continuous with *while* for the longer event. Use the simple past for the shorter event.
Note: You can reverse the two clauses, but you need a comma if the *while* clause comes first.

UNIT 4

Information Questions

Location	Where	is the bank?
	How far	is the school from here?
	What	is the address?
Time	When	does the library open?
	What time	does the restaurant close?
	How often	do the buses run?
Cost	How much	does it cost?

Adverbial Clauses with *Before, After* and *When*

Rule	Example
A comma separates an adverbial clause that comes before the main clause.	**Before** I went grocery shopping, I stopped by the cleaners to pick up some skirts. **After** I returned the books, I stopped by the bank to make a deposit. **When** everyone left the house, I made my list of errands.
A comma is not used when the adverbial clause comes after the main clause.	I stopped by the cleaners to pick up some skirts **before** I went grocery shopping. I stopped by the bank to make a deposit **after** I returned the books. I made my list of errands **when** everyone left the house.

UNIT 5

Present Perfect					
Subject	*Have*	Past Participle	Illness	Time	Example Sentence
I / You / We / They	have	been felt	sick ill	since Tuesday.	I **have been** sick **since** Tuesday.
She / He / It	has	had	a backache a headache	for two weeks.	She **has had** a backache **for** two weeks.
Use the present perfect for events starting in the past and continuing up to the present.					

Future Conditional Statements	
Cause: *If* + Present	Effect: Future
If you **are** very stressed,	you **will have** high blood pressure.
If you **don't get** enough calcium,	you **won't have** strong bones.
We can connect a cause and an effect by using a *future conditional* statement. The *if*-clause (or the *cause*) is in the present and the *effect* is in the future.	
Effect: Future	Cause: *if* + Present
You **will have** high blood pressure	**if** you **are** very stressed.
You can reverse the clauses, but use a comma only when the *if*-clause comes first.	

UNIT 6

Infinitives and Gerunds Infinitive = *to* + Verb Gerund = Verb + *ing*			
Verb	Infinitive or Gerund	Example Sentence	Other Verbs That Follow the Same Rule
want	infinitive	He wants **to get** a job.	plan, decide
enjoy	gerund	He enjoys **fixing** bicycles.	finish, give up
like	both	He likes **to talk.** He likes **talking.**	love, hate
Some verbs take the infinitive and some verbs take the gerund. There are some verbs that take both.			

Gerunds and Nouns after Prepositions					
Subject	Verb	Adjective	Preposition	Gerund / Noun	Example Sentence
I	am	good	at	fixing	I am good at **fixing** bycicles.
She	is	good	at	math	She is good at **math.**
A gerund or a noun follows an adjective + a preposition. Some other examples of adjectives + prepositions are *interested in, afraid of, tired of, bad at,* and *worried about.* When a noun is plural, it is also common to use the preposition *with: I am good with customers.*					

Would Rather					
Subject	*Would Rather*	**Base Form**	*Than*	**Base Form**	**Example Sentence**
I / You She / He / It We /They	would ('d) rather	work alone	than	work with people	I would rather work alone than work with people.
Note: You can omit the second verb if it is the same as the first verb: *I would rather work nights than (work) days.*					

UNIT 7

Review: Possessive Adjectives and Possessive Pronouns			
Possessive Adjectives	**Rule**		
my / your / his / her / its our / their	Possessive adjectives show possession of an object and come before the noun.		
Example Sentence			
Subject	**Verb**	**Possessive Adjective**	**Object**
This	is	**her**	office.
Possessive Pronouns	**Rule**		
mine / yours / his / /hers / its ours / theirs	Possessive pronouns show possession of an object and act as a noun.		
Example Sentence			
Subject	**Noun**	**Verb**	**Possessive Pronoun**
This	office	is	**hers.**

Modals: *Could* and *Might*			
Subject	**Modal**	**Verb**	**Example Sentence**
I / You / He / She It / We / They	could	fall.	You **could fall.**
	might	miss.	I **might miss** work.
The modals *could* and *might* are used interchangeably because they have a similar meaning when predicting future possibilities. We use them to say that there is a chance that something will happen in the future.			

UNIT 8

Comparing and Contrasting Ideas		
If two people share the same opinion, use *both . . . and* or *neither . . . nor*.		
Both	Enrico **and** Liz	want to increase the number of students in our class.
Neither	Suzanna **nor** Ali	wants to increase the number of students in our class.
If two people don't share the same opinion, use *but* or *however*.		
Enrico agrees with bilingual education,	**but** Liz doesn't.	
Ali doesn't agree with bilingual education;	**however**, Suzanna does.	
Punctuation Note: Use a semicolon (;) before and a comma (,) after *however*.		

Modal *Should*			
Subject	**Should**	**Base Verb**	
The city council	should	set	a curfew for teenagers.
People	should	clean up	after their pets.

Contrary-to-Fact Conditional Statements					
If	**Subject**	**Simple Past Verb + Noun**	**Subject**	**Modal**	**Base Verb + Noun**
If	I	had more money,	I	would	buy a house.
If	you	didn't have the flu,	you	would	go to work.
If	he	had more time,	he	would	take more classes.
If	she	were rich,	she	could	help her parents.
If	we	gave food to charities,	we	could	help our community.
If	they	weren't so tired,	they	could	come to the movies.
Contrary-to-fact (or unreal) conditional statements are sentences that are not true and that the speaker thinks will probably never be true. Note: In written English, we use *were* instead of *was* in contrary-to-fact statements, but in spoken English, we often use *was* with the following subjects: I, he, she, and it.					

Credits

ILLUSTRATIONS: Illustrations created by Oscar Hernandez. All illustrations and graphics are owned by © Cengage Learning, Inc.

Stand Out Skills Index

ACADEMIC SKILLS

Active Listening, 35, 61, 87, 113, 141, 167, 193, 219

Charts, tables, and maps, 4–5, 9–11, 14–16, 19, 26, 28, 30, 32–33, 40–41, 45–48, 50–51, 55–57, 67, 70, 74, 76, 79, 82–83, 88, 93–94, 97–99, 102, 107–108, 113, 124-125, 127–130, 135–137, 140, 149–151, 153, 159–162, 172–173, 178, 182, 185, 187–188, 198–199, 201–202, 206, 208, 211–217

Collaborate, 35, 61, 87, 113, 141, 167, 193, 219

Critical thinking
analyze, 7, 14, 20, 22, 36, 55, 80, 88, 102, 107, 126, 130, 142, 146, 156, 163, 172, 174, 179, 214, 220
apply, 5, 19, 42, 45, 48, 51, 53–54, 77, 80, 94, 103, 151, 157
assess, 163
brainstorm, 213
calculate, 177
categorize, 187
choose, 220
classify, 19, 40
collaborate, 87, 167
compare, 8, 10, 23, 25, 50, 55, 67, 83, 109, 172, 201, 203
compose, 8, 11, 54, 106
construct, 70
create, 16, 97, 154
decide, 95, 167
demonstrate, 92
determine, 78, 80, 92, 94, 154–155, 159, 199, 204
describe, 46, 125, 199, 204
discuss, 27
evaluate, 44, 47, 74, 82, 88, 128, 130, 149, 151, 154, 178, 206
expand, 62
explain, 41, 66, 134, 158, 201
find out, 3, 43, 202
formulate, 105, 209
generate, 180, 208
identify, 18, 46, 49, 148
illustrate, 76–77
infer, 88, 96, 162, 168, 194
interpret, 15, 24, 29, 43, 57, 69, 72–73, 75, 108, 153, 184, 189

justify, 45
locate, 198
plan, 131, 210
predict, 9, 36, 62, 142, 183–184
prepare, 160
put in order, 101
recall, 120
reflect, 28, 30, 36, 56, 163, 168, 189, 213
restate, 6
scan, 68, 220
sequence, 52, 62, 104
skim, 31
suggest, 12, 150
summarize, 134
survey, 4
visualize, 71, 212

Drawing
Maps, 111

Grammar
Adverbial clauses, 102–103, 111
be, 79
Comparative adjectives, 46–48, 51
Conditional statements, 127–128, 211, 218
Contrary–to–fact conditionals, 211, 218
could and *might*, 182–183
Frequency adverbs, 15–16, 32
Future conditional statements, 127–128
Future time clauses, 19
Gerunds, 150–151
Infinitives, 150
Information questions, 74, 93
Modals, 182
must vs. *have to*, 50–51, 60
Past continuous, 79, 86
Possessive adjectives, 173
Possessive pronouns, 173–174
Prepositions, 151
Present perfect, 124–125, 138
Requests, 185–186, 192
Sequencing transitions, 53–54, 60
should, 208, 217
Superlatives, 48, 67–68
while, 79
Yes / No questions, 70–71, 85

Group activities, 19, 29, 54–55, 97, 107, 148, 162, 174, 180, 183, 194, 206, 208–209, 220

Listening
Banking habits, 95
Bill paying, 75
Communication at work, 186
Company benefits, 179
Conversations, 73–74, 172, 186
Goals, obstacles, and solutions, 18
Greetings, 5
Housing, 69
Job interviews, 158
Nutritional information, 130
Purchasing methods, 50
Property management, 81
Study habits, 23
Time management, 26–27
To Do list, 92
US geography, 200
US government, 204, 206

Matching
Diseases, 122
Doctors, 121, 138
Employee benefits, 190
Health habits, 126
Job applications, 155
Job descriptions, 147
Job statistics, 81
Paragraph components, 33
Problems and solutions, 78, 208
Questions and answers, 93–94
Study habits, 25
Symbols, 98
US geography, 200

Partner activities, 4–5, 8, 10, 16, 20, 23, 25, 32, 36, 42, 47–48, 50, 55–56, 66–72, 74–76, 78, 80, 83, 92–95, 99–100, 102–103, 109, 111–112, 114, 120–122, 128, 130–132, 134, 136–137, 140, 146, 148–149, 151, 155, 158, 160–161, 166, 172, 174, 176, 178, 181, 186, 188, 190, 192, 199, 201–202, 208, 211, 213

Presentation, 35, 61, 87, 113, 141, 167, 193, 219

Pronunciation
Contractions, 4
Information questions, 93
Making requests, 175¡
Pausing, 103

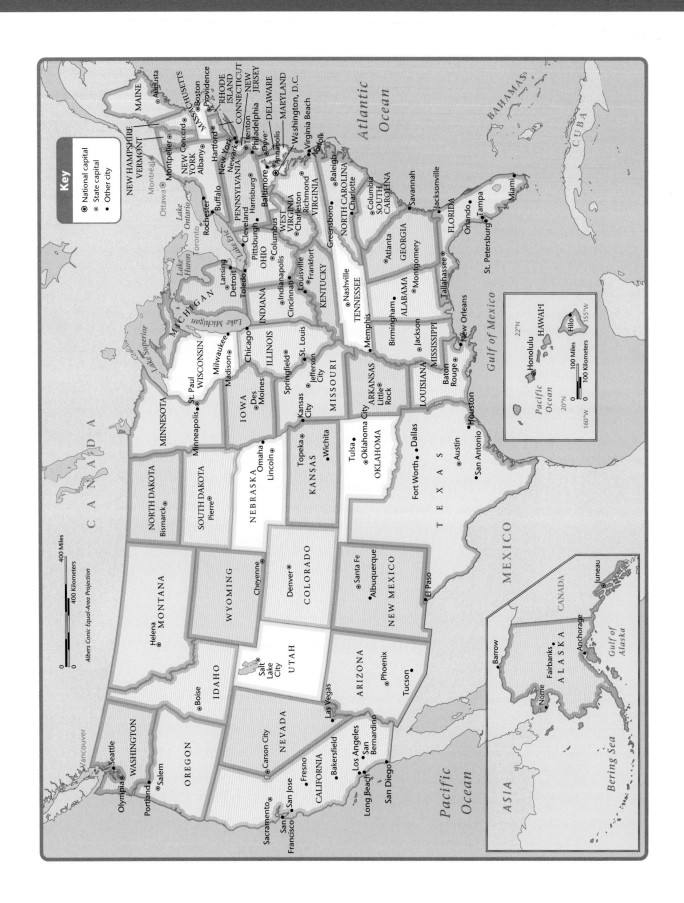